"I have been taking retreats for most of my adult life—how I wish I had this book long ago to guide me! Ruth provides practical ways to make our time alone with God much more intentional and ultimately more life giving. After I put the book down, I was ready to schedule a retreat armed with a whole new perspective and plan."

Nancy Beach, leadership coach with Slingshot Group, author of *Gifted to Lead: The Art of Leading as a Woman in the Church*

"I have had the privilege of being on retreat with Ruth as she led with a passion and patience that refueled us weary travelers on the faith journey. If you are desperate to meet God, start with this book. *Invitation to Retreat* forced me to accept a truth all Christians must grapple with: unless we retreat into solitude and silence to be alone with our God, we will never have a real relationship with him. We will spend our lives believing we have a relationship because we go to church, hear about God from others, read and study about God, even hang theological diplomas on our walls. Yet even then, we may not *know* him. This book is an invitation into the process and the practice of building intentional rhythms into this busy life of ours—to simply be with the One who loved us first and *actually have* a relationship with God."

Ricky Staub, founder of Neighborhood Film Company

"A wise new guide to retreat dealing not just with practical questions on how but the even more significant why. Ruth Haley Barton reminds us we need to pause, rest, relent, and let God take charge. She mentions many guides and wisdom figures, but the best is God's Spirit working in us when we let go. I was struck by her final chapter about coming back from retreat strengthened to bless others who need our counsel. *Invitation to Retreat* is powerful."

Emilie Griffin, author of *Wilderness Time* and *Doors into Prayer*

"Early on in Ruth Haley Barton's *Invitation to Retreat*, she levels the chilling diagnosis: 'If we are honest, many of us have given up hope that we will ever be rested.' Far from hopeless, however, Ruth lays out the comprehensive antidote. From her insightful analysis of just what is making us so tired, to her incredibly inviting description of 'strategic withdrawal,' to the copious practical retreat materials and suggestions, this book might be the first thing you pack for your next retreat. Like a consummate wilderness guide, Ruth paints an enticing picture of the destination then patiently leads us every step of the way."

Jim Martin, vice president of spiritual formation at International Justice Mission, author of *The Just Church*

"Ruth is one of single greatest gifts God has brought into my life, and I believe she is a prophetic voice bringing healing and hope to pastors and leaders that are desperate to find rest. Ruth speaks from a deep and authentic well. She has done her own work in creating rhythms of rest that relinquish control, respond to the voice of God, and recalibrate life so she is healthy and whole. You hold in your hands one of the most impactful books I have read."

Jeanne Stevens, lead pastor at Soul City Church

"I have had the great privilege of attending retreats led by Ruth Haley Barton on more than a dozen occasions. Because she knows the demands of ministry firsthand, her invitation for pastors and leaders to retreat is an urgent one, with a singular focus: to have a fresh encounter with God for our own soul's sake. *Invitation to Retreat* lays a foundation for the necessity of retreat, but it also serves as a guide for those who have the courage to accept the invitation itself."

Steve Wiens, author of *Beginnings* and senior pastor of Genesis Covenant Church in Robbinsdale, Minnesota

"This book offers practical guidance and astonishing insight into the physical, psychological, and spiritual dynamics of intentional solitude. Thank you, Ruth Haley Barton, for sharing your well-earned wisdom about listening to the heart of the Creator and the authentic self."

Mark Scandrette, founding director of ReIMAGINE, coauthor of *Free* and *Belonging and Becoming*

"Many years ago when I was just a few years into ministry, I took my first spiritual retreat. . . . Since that first retreat to this very day, Ruth has been a friend, mentor, and advocate for my soul. . . . [This book] is an echo of the invitation given by Jesus to simply 'come with me by yourselves to a quiet place and get some rest.' You need this book more than you know. Trust me. You do. And if you are willing to say yes to this invitation to retreat, I believe that you will find a burden that is far lighter than you have made it and a Savior who is far closer than you imagined."

Jarrett Stevens, copastor of Soul City Church, author of *Four Small Words*

"When Ruth Haley Barton shared her new manuscript with me for *Invitation to Retreat*, I knew it would prove to be another powerful tool to enjoy and experience the presence of God. However, I was unprepared for such practical, honest, and open insights into the spiritual discipline of retreat. If we're serious about true spiritual transformation, I would encourage all of us to explore God's invitation to get away, rest, and reflect through the pages of this book."

Santiago "Jimmy" Mellado, president and CEO, Compassion International

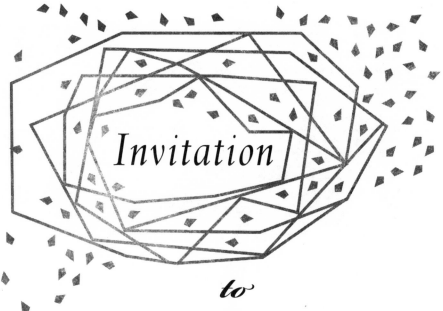

Invitation

to

RETREAT

The Gift and Necessity of Time Away with God

RUTH HALEY BARTON

IVP Books

An imprint of InterVarsity Press
Downers Grove, Illinois

BV
5068
.R4
B37
2018

InterVarsity Press
P.O. Box 1400, Downers Grove, IL 60515-1426
ivpress.com
email@ivpress.com

©2018 by Ruth Haley Barton

All rights reserved. No part of this book may be reproduced in any form without written permission from InterVarsity Press.

InterVarsity Press® is the book-publishing division of InterVarsity Christian Fellowship/USA®, a movement of students and faculty active on campus at hundreds of universities, colleges, and schools of nursing in the United States of America, and a member movement of the International Fellowship of Evangelical Students. For information about local and regional activities, visit intervarsity.org.

Scripture quotations, unless otherwise noted, are from the New Revised Standard Version of the Bible, copyright 1989 by the Division of Christian Education of the National Council of the Churches of Christ in the USA. Used by permission. All rights reserved.

While any stories in this book are true, some names and identifying information may have been changed to protect the privacy of individuals.

"Sometimes" by David Whyte is printed with permission from Many Rivers Press, www.davidwhyte.com. David Whyte, "Sometimes," Everyting Is Waiting for You (Langley, WA: Many Rivers Press, 2003).

Cover design: David Fassett
Interior design: Jeanna Wiggins
Images: winter painted background: © Pobytov / Digital Vision Vectors / Getty Images
gold textured background: © letoosen / iStock / Getty Images Plus
glittering background: © oatawa / iStock / Getty Images Plus
white textured paper: © xamtiw / iStock / Getty Images Plus
abstract blue background: © Pobytov / Digital Vision Vectors / Getty Images
gold textured background: © FrankvandenBergh / E+ / Getty Images
blurred pastel background: © NYS444 / iStock / Getty Images Plus
liquid marble pattern: © anyababii / iStock / Getty Images Plus
abstract blue watercolor: © kostins / iStock / Getty Images Plus

ISBN 978-0-8308-4646-7 (print)
ISBN 978-0-8308-7393-7 (digital)

Printed in Canada ∞

InterVarsity Press is committed to ecological stewardship and to the conservation of natural resources in all our operations. This book was printed using sustainably sourced paper.

Library of Congress Cataloging-in-Publication Data
Names: Barton, R. Ruth, 1960- author.
Title: Invitation to retreat : the gift and necessity of time away with God /
Ruth Haley Barton.
Description: Downers Grove : InterVarsity Press, 2018. | Includes
bibliographical references.
Identifiers: LCCN 2018017719 (print) | LCCN 2018025653 (ebook) | ISBN
9780830873937 (eBook) | ISBN 9780830846467 (hardcover : alk. paper)
Subjects: LCSH: Spiritual retreats—Christianity. | Spiritual
life—Christianity.
Classification: LCC BV5068.R4 (ebook) | LCC BV5068.R4 B37 2018 (print) | DDC
269/.6—dc23
LC record available at https://lccn.loc.gov/2018017719

P	23	22	21	20	19	18	17	16	15	14	13	12	11	10	9	8	7	6	5	4	3	2	1
Y	37	36	35	34	33	32	31	30	29	28	27	26	25	24	23	22	21	20	19	18

To Fr. Eric Jensen, SJ

The right spiritual director at the right time.

Thanks be to God!

❦

And to my mom,

JoAnn Neburka Haley

(July 17, 1934–December 24, 2017),

who entered into her final rest

just as I was finishing the book.

You are now fully experiencing what

I can only babble about.

CONTENTS

Oh God of peace,

who has taught us that in returning and rest

we shall be saved,

in quietness and trust shall be our strength;

By the power of your Holy Spirit

quiet our hearts we pray,

that we may be still and know that you are God,

through Jesus Christ our Lord.

Amen.

THE BOOK OF COMMON PRAYER

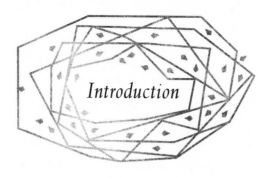

Introduction

INVITATION
to RETREAT

If you don't come apart for a while,
you will come apart after a while.

DALLAS WILLARD

⬧ ⬧ ⬧

I T IS A WONDERFUL THING TO BE INVITED—especially when the
invitation is particularly well-suited to our needs, our desires, our
delights. A gifted communicator receives a significant invitation to
speak on a topic that is important to them. An artist is commissioned
to create banners for the Easter processional or design a memorial that
will forever commemorate a historic event. A pastor gets called to
serve a church that they feel drawn to. Your family gets invited to
another family's home for Thanksgiving or Christmas dinner. A man
invites a woman to marry him—or vice versa!

When it's the right invitation, we feel honored, we feel warmed, we
feel drawn. Everything in us leaps to say yes!

TIRED OF BEING TOLD WHAT TO DO

One of the reasons I love a good invitation is that I get tired of being told what to do. As the *very* responsible oldest daughter of a pastor and someone who entered vocational ministry at a young age, my life has been shaped by a strong sense of what I had to do, what I needed to do, and what I ought to do, according to a lot of other people's expectations. And there is nothing wrong with that, as far as it goes. But these days I find a good invitation to be much more compelling than responsibility. To be *invited* into something that is right for me and to have the chance to choose freely, well, that is an entirely different experience! With a true invitation, there is no coercion, no forcing, no guilting, no manipulation—just a winsome opportunity, an openhearted welcome and the freedom to say yes or no.

An invitation means that I really do have a choice, and I just love that!

The other thing that is simply wonderful about a good invitation is that it means I am wanted. For some of us the desire to be wanted is closer to the surface than it is for others, but no matter how buried it might be, the desire to know we are appreciated, accepted, and desired is a fairly universal human longing. Our awareness of this longing and our experiences with how this desire was met (or not) go way back and may shape us even now. We all have early memories of knowing something special was going on—a bunch of girls having a sleepover, a birthday party for one of the cool kids, a group of guys playing baseball or street hockey—and experiencing the sting of realizing we were not invited. We might remember the grade school excitement of being invited to someone's house after school and looking forward to it all day *or* the sting of not being invited when others have been.

As we grew into adolescence, we may have felt the security of being included in a group of good friends or the emptiness of being on the outside. We might have waited breathlessly for an invitation to an upcoming dance, *or* we may have been the one doing the asking and waiting breathlessly for that person's response. Perhaps we yearned to be part of the cast for a major production, to be on the football team, or even invited to be a special helper to a teacher we liked. Whatever our experiences have been, we know *instinctively* that to be invited means we are wanted and, in the very best scenario, wanted by someone we find interesting, intriguing, or just plain cool. And that is exactly what makes the invitation to retreat so compelling. It is a winsome call from this intriguing person we call God—the One who loves us, the One who is inexplicably drawn to us, the One who knows so intimately what we need in order to be well. It is an invitation straight from the heart of Jesus to us—his enthusiastic disciples who routinely wear ourselves out with good things and with lesser things, and we don't even know we're doing it half the time! Taking on too much at work without prioritizing, thinking I can be the savior of all who are convinced they need time with me, making commitments I cannot possibly keep without running myself into the ground, reacting and responding to every need as though it were mine to fix, trying to be perfect and never disappoint—all of these compulsive behaviors ensure I will never come away and rest awhile.

Imagine the disciples' surprise in Mark 6:30-31 when, in the midst of their excitement about "all they had done and taught" in Jesus' name, he invited them to retreat. Literally! His words, "Come away to a deserted place . . . and rest a while," shut down the conversation the disciples wanted to have and redirected it to the conversation Jesus wanted to have—about retreat! I can see them ceasing their breathless chatter, cocking their heads a bit in disbelief and thinking, *Well, that's different!* What a wonder it is, as Jesus' disciples, to be invited by him to conversation and communion, self-care and replenishment.

RECLAIMING RETREAT AS A SPIRITUAL PRACTICE

The problem with trying to talk about retreat these days is that the word itself has been severely compromised, both in the secular culture and in the religious subculture. In business circles, a retreat is often a long meeting from which you cannot go home. It usually involves extended days spent off-site in which the event organizers not only have control over your daytime working hours but also your evening and early morning hours. Typically, we work harder on "retreat" than in our normal working days, and of course we come home exhausted.

The same is true in church culture. A retreat might involve an extended time away for the elders or pastoral staff to do strategic planning or problem solving. Usually time is built in for fellowship and community building, which means that the days are long and the evenings even longer!

We also might be accustomed to youth retreats and men's, women's, or couple's retreats that include multiple teaching sessions with many other carefully orchestrated programming elements—loud music, icebreakers, games, elective workshops, activities, skits, and entertainment. Participants typically share rooms, which means they stay up later than usual and don't rest as well because of the snoring person in the other bed! While such events are wonderful opportunities for building community and creating space for focused teaching and interaction with others, they can also be stimulating to the extent that no one leaves rested or in touch with their own souls—at least not in the way Jesus encouraged his disciples to "come away with me and rest a while."

So what are we really talking about when we reference retreat as a spiritual practice?

A GENEROUS COMMITMENT TO
OUR FRIENDSHIP WITH GOD

Retreat in the context of the spiritual life is an *extended time apart* for the purpose of being with God and giving God our full and undivided attention; it is, as Emilie Griffin puts it, "a generous commitment to our friendship with God." The emphasis is on the words *extended* and *generous.* Truth is, we are not always generous with ourselves where God is concerned. Many of us have done well to incorporate regular times of solitude and silence into the rhythm of our ordinary lives, which means we've gotten pretty good at giving God twenty minutes here and half an hour there. And there's no question we are better for it!

But many of us are longing for more—and we have a sense that there *is* more if we could create more space for quiet to give attention to God at the center of our beings. We sense that a kind of fullness and satisfaction is discovered more in the silence than in the words, more in solitude than in socializing, more in spaciousness than in busyness. "Times come," Emilie Griffin goes on to say, "when we yearn for more of God than our schedules will allow. We are tired, we are crushed, we are crowded by friends and acquaintances, commitments and obligations. The life of grace is abounding, but we are too busy for it. Even good obligations begin to hem us in."

Ron Roheiser points out three images for retreat used in Scripture that meet us in our yearning; all of them apply in different ways at different times.

- There is the lonely place to which Jesus invited his disciples when he said, "Come away to a deserted place . . . and rest a while" (Mark 6:30). With this invitation he was calling them out of their busyness to a place of rest beyond the demands of their life in ministry, as we referenced earlier.

- There is the desert/wilderness that the Spirit drove Jesus to after his baptism (Luke 4). Here he did battle with Satan and faced his demons, as we all must. But there's more! Old Testament references hint at the fact that the wilderness (spiritually speaking) is also a place of intimacy where God tenderly speaks those things he has been wanting to say to our souls: "Therefore I will now allure her, / and bring her into the wilderness / and speak tenderly to her. . . . / There she shall respond as in the days of her youth" (Hosea 2:14-15). "When Israel was a child, I loved him, / and out of Egypt I called my son [to a journey through the wilderness to the Promised Land]. / The more I called them, / the more they went from me" (Hosea 11:1-2). Clearly something special happens between God and his people in the wilderness!

- And there is the Sabbath, the first retreat of all retreats, in which God introduces rhythms of work and rest to the way we order our time. When time had no shape at all, God—by his example and by his instruction—established optimal rhythms for his creation that included working six days and resting on the seventh. This was not a lifestyle suggestion; it was a commandment as significant as not murdering, not committing adultery, and not lying.

There has never been a time when the invitation to retreat is so radical and so relevant, so needed and so welcome.

These metaphors form the biblical/spiritual context for reclaiming retreat as spiritual practice for our time. In fact, there has never been a time when the invitation to retreat is so radical and so relevant, so needed and so welcome.

A COUNTERCULTURAL PRACTICE

The yearning for retreat: Can you feel it? That yearning is your invitation. It is the Spirit of God stirring up your deepest longings and questions in order to draw you deeper into the intimacy with the God you were created for. Will you trust it? Are you brave enough to let it carry you into the *more*?

To fully reclaim retreat as a practice that will open us to God, we will explore some of the concrete invitations contained within the more general one. We will consider the meaning of a *military retreat* (otherwise known as "strategic withdrawal") for our own lives—

putting distance between ourselves and the battle line, wherever that line is drawn in our lives right now. We will hear God's invitation to *rest* and learn what we must *relinquish* in order to do that. We will experience *rhythms* that *replenish* us—body, mind, and soul. We will practice *recognizing* and *responding* to the presence of God through discernment, and *recalibrate* based on what God is saying to our souls. We will feel ourselves drawn to *reengage* our lives in the company of others from a more rested place and establish regular patterns of *returning* and *resting* in God.

You can use this book to prepare for a variety of types of retreats. For example, it will help you to be ready for a group retreat in which you are provided with a schedule and content for your time. But it will also be company for you if you are making a solitary venture into retreat. Likewise, you can read this book ahead of your retreat, using the ideas at the end of each chapter under the heading "Preparing for Retreat," or you can take it with you and read it when you get there, using the ideas under the heading "While on Retreat." Whatever you do, don't let this book itself become a burden or type of homework that actually keeps you from entering in. God will always be willing to meet you if you show up with an open heart.

My guess is that the invitation to retreat feels as different and countercultural to most of us as it felt to the disciples, but it was—and is!—the right invitation, offered by One who knows his children so well. The *beauty* of it is that we are not pushed, coerced, manipulated, or told we have to. Rather, we are invited to enter into something so good for us—body, mind, and soul—that once we recognize it as the winsome opportunity it really is, everything in us will leap to say yes. We may even wonder why it took us so long!

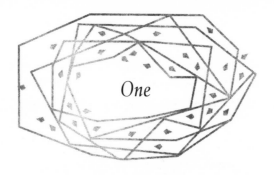

One

STRATEGIC
WITHDRAWAL

I have lived too long where I am reachable.

RUMI

BRAD IS A PASTOR WHOSE CHURCH IS GOING WELL. Attendance at weekend services is growing steadily, and they have just completed a building project that is enabling them to grow and provide a variety of ministries to meet needs within their growing congregation and the community surrounding them. People respond well to his preaching, and his church is known around town as being a church that cares. Brad is growing in stature and reputation among local leaders—even becoming a respected voice regarding important issues facing the community—which means he is in demand and attends many meetings. He is increasingly aware that it takes a full-time schedule and more to keep all the plates spinning. His two young children could use much more attention than he able to give them, and his wife is exhausted from picking up the slack from his busy schedule. When he looks in her eyes he sees a hollowness that mirrors the emptiness he feels in his own soul, but the demands of being a young pastor whose star is rising, the husband and father of growing family, and a soul that is longing for more seem mutually exclusive.

Jen is a stay-at-home mom with four kids. She loves being a mom and sees this as her highest priority, yet over the years she has had a niggling sense that there is something more she is supposed to do with herself and her gifts. Her husband travels regularly for work, which means the lion's share of care for home and family falls to her; she has little time to devote to getting in touch with her spiritual desires and her sense of calling. Most of the time she is able to put aside her questions and desires in order to make sure everyone else's needs are cared for, but lately they have been pressing in on her. She finds herself close to tears a lot, questioning her worth, questioning her motives, and wondering if she is doing enough for all the people who need her. She feels her sense of self slipping away and is alarmed by feelings of anger, unsettledness, and even depression.

Jeremy is a gifted entrepreneur who is just starting to achieve recognition for the work his creative company is offering. The phone is ringing with offers of more work than their company can handle, and they have even received a few awards for their work. At the same time, there are internal problems in the company—dissension in the ranks, stress fractures in the leadership, and temptations when he travels. Given the external accolades, he cannot understand why things feel so broken on the inside. He realizes that if he does not get some time away to reflect on what's really going on, to listen to God, and to get a handle on his motivations and behaviors, he may ruin everything he's worked so hard for due to bad decision making— decision making that is disconnected from discerning God's presence and activity in his life.

PULLING BACK FROM DANGER

When we hear the word *retreat* many of us think of the military use of the word, which refers to the tactic troops use when they are losing too much ground, when they are tired and ineffective, and when there have been too many casualties or the current strategy is not working. When any of these scenarios are in play, the commander might instruct the troops to pull back and put some distance between themselves and the battle line. We often see this as a negative thing; however, military retreat can also be a wise tactic—an opportunity to rest the troops and tend to their wounds, to stop the enemy's momentum, or to step back to get a panoramic view of what's going and set new strategies. In fact, the military is now using a more positive term—*strategic withdrawal*—to describe retreat, and I like it!

Strategic withdrawal captures the more positive connotations of the word *retreat*, namely, that there are times when the better part of wisdom in combat *is* to withdraw for good reasons—which can apply to us as well. There are times when we too need to pull back from the battle line in own lives rather than continuing to fight the same battles in the same old ways. We need to pull back from our busyness, from life in our culture, from other people's expectations and our own compulsions, from whatever is not working in our lives.

The other thing that is true for those of us who have been walking with God for a long time is that all of us have either sustained real wounds in the battle of life or we're just plain tired. Many of us just soldier on, hoping time will heal all things. But experience tells us that while time does stop the bleeding and heals our wounds, scar tissue often remains. While on the surface it might seem like all is well, a hardening has taken place; ironically, those tight, hurting places are tender and can flare with pain when touched in the wrong way by some unsuspecting soul. And there might be numb places where we cannot feel anything at all.

At some point in our Christian life, many of us realize no one ever told us how to deal with our wounds that are still there—buried deeper than ever—but still there. Father Ronald Rolheiser aptly describes this dawning awareness:

> Once the sheer impulse of life begins to be tempered by the weight of our commitments and the grind of the years, more of our sensitivities begin to break through, and we sense more and more how we have been wounded and how life has not been fair to us. New demons then emerge: bitterness, anger, jealousy, and a sense of how we have been cheated. Disappointment cools the fiery energies of our youth, and our enthusiasm begins to be tempered by bitterness and anger . . . where once we struggled to properly control our energies, we now struggle to access them.

The point is that the evil one is never done stirring up trouble up and instigating new skirmishes. No matter how far along we are in the spiritual life, there is no time when retreat—or strategic withdrawal—ceases to be an essential practice. The battle lines might be drawn in different places at different stages of our lives, but retreat is always a practice we can engage when we too are tired or wounded, lacking in wisdom, or seeking more effective approaches to engaging the fight. Retreat is a time when we are strengthened for battle, putting on the whole armor of God that Paul describes so specifically (Ephesians 6:10-17).

No matter how far along we are in the spiritual life, there is no time when retreat —or strategic withdrawal—ceases to be an essential practice.

While it might seem strange to begin our reflections on such a gentle topic with such a harsh metaphor, the truth is there are times when the invitation to strategic withdrawal is exactly what we most need!

ON THE FRONT LINES OF A SPIRITUAL BATTLE

So much about the military tactic of retreat is applicable to Christians. If we are following Jesus—especially if we are trying to serve meaningfully in Christ's kingdom or exercising any kind of spiritual leadership—there is no question we are on the front lines of a spiritual battle. Ephesians 6:12, in particular, reminds us that we are engaged in a spiritual conflict with the evil one: "Our struggle is not against enemies of blood and flesh," Paul says, "but against the rulers, against the authorities, against the cosmic powers of this present darkness, against the spiritual forces of evil in the heavenly places."

Paul describes the Christian life in rather dramatic terms as a battle in which the evil one attacks us with flaming arrows. Paul's counsel in the face of this reality is that we must stand firm and confront these deadly forces by putting on the whole armor of God—which he then describes in detail.

While I am not one to see a demon behind every bush or spiritual warfare in every difficulty, the fact is that we are regularly engaged in the struggle against good and evil—whether we know it or not. And as we mature in our faith, the battles become more subtle and hard to detect: the good is often the enemy of the best and it is hard to know the difference. Of necessity, the weapons of our warfare must become more precise as well.

A point may come on the spiritual journey when persons who deeply love God must be aware of, understand, and reject certain attractions to *good and holy things* that, if undertaken, would distract them from the different good and holy things to which God is genuinely calling them. . . . They will need to discern between spiritual consolation that is authentically of the good spirit and deceptive spiritual consolation that is not of the good spirit, and that will lead, if followed, to spiritual harm.

I will say more about discernment later on, but for now it is enough to note that the military definition of *retreat* as "strategic withdrawal" fits this reality of the spiritual life quite well. There comes a time when the Christian who is awake and aware notices that the battle is different than it used to be, and the battle lines are drawn in different places. Satan's tactics are even more devious and hard to recognize than they were earlier in our life, and the weapons of our warfare must be wielded differently. Such times can actually be quite confusing, and wisdom whispers deep in our souls that we must pull back in order to gain perspective and set new strategies.

WHERE AM I IN DANGER?

The first invitation contained in the more general invitation to retreat is to notice where our lives might be in danger—to identify where the spiritual battle is raging—and to pull back so we can rest, heal, and set new strategies before reengaging. When in the middle of a battle, retreating can feel like a radical and counterintuitive choice—like we are actually ensuring our own defeat.

Some of us are reticent to walk away from a battle that is still in progress, accustomed as we are to stand our ground, swinging, whether it's doing any good or not! At such moments we may be convinced that the battle will be won or lost on the basis of our ability to keep fighting, when in truth, "the battle is the Lord's" as the Scriptures tell us. Retreat is an opportunity to act like we really believe this!

Others of us are more accustomed to avoiding the battle by pretending there isn't one! Perhaps we believe that if we don't acknowledge it or engage it, maybe it will simply go away. If this is our tendency, retreat is an opportunity to act like we believe the truth of Ephesians 6—that there really is a battle, that it is a serious one, and that none of us can fight 24/7. There comes a time when soldiers who have been involved in a real battle need to take a break—to rest, to allow God to tend our wounds, to get a perspective, and to review the battle from that perspective, inviting God to give us the wisdom we need.

Neither of those approaches—relying on ourselves to fight the good fight 24/7 or pretending there is no battle and avoiding it altogether—is an effective way to approach the rigors of the spiritual life. If we accept the military definition of *retreat* as an appropriate one for us as Christians, it might lead us to wonder, *Where am I in danger in my life right now?* Not only does this question orient us toward our need for retreat, it can also help us shape our retreat time in ways that correspond to the dangers we are experiencing currently. This question is always relevant, since the battle line is always shifting, and there are so many different ways we can be in danger—even in the relative safety in which most of us live.

ON THE BRINK OF DISASTER

In a recent article titled (disturbingly) "I Used to Be a Human Being," Andrew Sullivan offers an insightful description of how he arrived at an extended retreat after finding himself in danger due to his constant engagement with technology. "A year before," he says,

> like many addicts, I had sensed a personal crash coming. For a decade and a half, I'd been a web obsessive, publishing blog posts multiple times a day, seven days a week, and ultimately corralling a team that curated the web every 20 minutes during peak hours. Each morning began with a full immersion in the stream of internet consciousness and news, jumping from site to site, tweet to tweet, breaking news story to hottest take, scanning countless images and videos, catching up with multiple memes. Throughout the day I'd cough up an insight or an argument or a joke about what had just occurred or what was happening right now. At times, I'd spend weeks manically grabbing every tiny scrap of a developing story in order to fuse them into a narrative in real

time. I was in an unending dialogue with readers who were cav-
iling, praising, booing, correcting. My brain had never been so
occupied so insistently by so many different subjects and in so
public a way for so long.

Sullivan goes on to describe, with alarming precision, his realization
that he had been engaging—like most addicts—in a form of denial about
how his addiction to technology and the web was affecting his life.

I began to realize, as my health and happiness deteriorated, that
this was not a both-and kind of situation. It was either-or. Every
hour I spent online was not spent in the physical world. Every
minute I was engrossed in a virtual interaction I was not involved in a human encounter. Every second absorbed in some
sort of trivia was a second less for any form of reflection, or calm
or spirituality. "Multitasking" was a mirage. This was a zero-sum
question. I either lived as a voice online or I lived as a human
being in the world that humans have lived in since the beginning
of time. And so I decided, after 15 years, to live in reality.

And so he "quit the web," throwing his life and his career up in the air.

DISTRACTED TO DEATH

Several months later, Sullivan arrived at a silent retreat, seeking the
ultimate detox. Unplugging completely enabled him to identify more
clearly what has been lost in our "always plugged in" culture and the
severity of the dangers of living such a life.

Information now penetrates every waking moment of our lives as
we are constantly being "guided to info-nuggets by myriad little interactions on social media, all cascading at us with individually tai-
lored relevance and accuracy. No information technology ever had
this depth of knowledge of its consumers—or greater capacity to
tweak their synapses to keep them in engaged." One of the results of

such overstimulation is reduced attention span, which is now well-documented by multiple sources. What's most disturbing is that I see myself in his description! I am alarmed by how often I—a lover of words and books, sustained thought and deep reflection, writing that emerges from being in touch with one's soul—give in to the constant tug and pull toward the ever-present stimulation provided by email, texting, Instagram, and the constant availability and intrusion of information from the web. I am saddened and concerned about the fact that whereas I used to be able to lose myself in reading, reflection, and writing, I now struggle to finish a longer journal article that has no pictures, attached videos, or clever sound-bites! This is not good!

As recently as ten years ago smartphones didn't even exist, but now, in less than a decade, these devices have gone from unknown to ubiquitous, unimaginable to indispensable. Wherever we look, people are "crouched over their phones as they walk the streets, or drive their cars, or walk their dogs, or play with their children. . . . We have gone from looking up and around to constantly looking down."

I'll never forget the first time I noticed this phenomenon for myself. On a stunningly beautiful spring day after a particularly brutal Chicago winter, I noticed several people walking their dogs. But the thing is, none of them were simply walking and taking in the beauty of the day, letting it restore their souls after the dark time we had just been through. *All* of them were on their cell phones! I felt something break inside me, like a valuable treasure had been lost and we might never get it back.

OUT OF TOUCH WITH OUR HUMAN EXISTENCE

On the third day of his retreat, Sullivan describes walking through the forest and being overcome by emotions regarding his painful childhood. Even though he was aware of the brokenness this had formed in him, which he had spent years trying to unravel and fix, on retreat he was present to his life and his emotional depths in a new way. He says,

> I had never felt it [the pain] so vividly since the very years it had first engulfed and defined me. It was as if, having slowly and progressively removed every distraction from my life, I was suddenly faced with what I had been distracting myself from. Resting for a moment against the trunk of a tree, I stopped and suddenly found myself bent over, convulsed with the newly present pain, sobbing.

While this might sound like being retraumatized, it was actually healing. A wise retreat guide reassured him: "Don't worry. Be patient. It will resolve itself." So he persevered in the quiet of being completely unplugged, and because he couldn't distract himself by checking email, refreshing Instagram, or looking at text messages, over time a different kind of resolution emerged from what he had experienced previously.

> Over the next day, the feelings began to ebb, my meditation practice began to improve, the sadness shifted into a kind of calm and rest. I felt other things from my childhood—the beauty of forests, the joy of friends, the support of my sister, the love of my maternal grandmother. Yes, I prayed, and prayed for relief. But this lifting felt like a normal process of revisiting and healing and recovering. It felt like an ancient long-buried gift.

One of the dangers of living in a constant state of distraction is that we never go to the bottom of our pain, our sadness, our emptiness, which means we never find that rock-bottom place of the peace that passes understanding and rest ourselves there. We never receive the comfort promised to those who mourn, so we are always on the prowl for more and better distractions. Not only are we distracted from the present, we are distracted from our very lives; we miss out on the comfort that is there for us when we are present to our own depths in God's presence.

STRANGE ISOLATION

While on retreat, Sullivan was able to acknowledge that even though he "had been accompanied for so long by verbal and visual noise" and "an endless bombardment of words and images," the truth is that he "felt curiously isolated." This is the strange phenomenon Sherry Turkle has described as being "alone together"—families together but not really together because everyone is on their devices, friends or colleagues trying to share time together or to have a meeting while everyone has at least one eye or ear tuned to whatever else might prove to be more important, conversations that stay on the surface because the phones on the table remind us that we are not really giving or getting each other's undivided attention.

Kara, in her fifties, offers this poignant observation about how life in her hometown of Portland, Maine, feels these days: "Sometimes I walk down the street, and I'm the only person not plugged in. . . . No one is where they are. They're talking to someone miles away. I miss them."

Recently a professor shared with me a college student's reflections in response to my earlier writings on solitude and silence:

I was not born into a world relatively unaffected by technology like you were. Rather, I was thrust into a world that had already succumbed to its disastrous effects! I have heard it said that the Internet was going to make the world a smaller place, and indeed it has. It has reduced the world from seven billion to just one! Just you, hiding behind your screen, interacting with others hiding behind theirs. The days of legitimate human interaction have been forever tainted by social media. The schedules of our workdays have been compressed tighter by the interventions of e-mails and cellphones. Our lives have been faker and faker, busier and busier and we have yet to realize that within, we are broken, weary and longing for that genuine, restful interaction that we find with God in solitude.

WHERE WE PUT OUR FAITH

Sullivan does not claim any sort of religious affiliation in his article, but, interestingly enough, he refers to the loss of faith as one consequence of being constantly connected and plugged in to whatever technology is serving up. I think he's on to something! While we may continue to affirm a particular set of theological beliefs, our addiction to technology indicates that in some ways we are putting our faith *there*. A case could be made that by giving so much of our time, attention, and priority to what takes place in and through technology, we are saying, "This is what interests me. This is what I most value. This is where I am searching for answers. This is what makes me feel okay. This is what will save me."

Sullivan then offers this bit of advice to the church.

> If the churches came to understand that the greatest threat to faith today is not hedonism but distraction, perhaps they might begin to appeal to a frazzled digital generation. Christian leaders seem to think that they need more distraction to counter the distraction. Their services have degenerated into emotional spasms, their spaces drowned with light and noise and locked shut throughout the day, when their darkness and silence might actually draw those whose minds and souls have grown web-weary. . . . This new epidemic of distraction is our civilization's specific weakness. And its threat is not so much to our minds, even as they shape-shift under pressure. The threat is to our souls. At this rate, if the noise does not relent, we might even forget we have any.

Sullivan is touching on a deep desire of serious spiritual seekers today. Many who are on an intentional spiritual journey—including myself—long for quiet spaces to connect with God and with their own souls as part of their church experience. We wonder, *Does our involvement with the church make us busier or better—the kind of better that comes from being open and receptive to God?* One of the reasons I am drawn to worship in more liturgical settings is that silence is often built into the church service, not to mention quiet spaces in the building that are open for reflection and prayer throughout the day. But here's the thing: even in churches where silence is written into the service, it's almost perfunctory. Thirty seconds at most! Just as my soul is settling into its natural state of silent presence to God, somebody starts talking again. Could we, as a matter of course, be still a little bit longer in church and experience *together* that God is God? Could moments of retreating from noise, words, and activity be built into our times together as faith communities?

Many who are on an intentional spiritual journey long for quiet spaces to connect with God and with their own souls.

Now there's some food for thought!

AM I FIGHTING THE RIGHT BATTLE?

I will never forget one pastor's comment after taking some time to reflect on the military aspects of the invitation to retreat. After emerging from solitude he commented ruefully, "In the silence, I realized that I'm not even sure I'm fighting the right battle. I just want to know I'm fighting the right battle."

Many of us are wasting our life's energy fighting for things that aren't that important in the whole scheme of things. There are times when the quiet of retreat is the only way we will be able to discern well what battle we should be engaging and how. As it turns out, the invitation to pull back and put some distance between ourselves and the battle line is the first and, in some ways, most significant invitation contained within the general invitation to retreat. Why?

Because if you don't say yes to this one, none of the rest of the invitations will be possible.

Practicing RETREAT

Preparing for retreat. The first move in the practice of retreat is to get yourself there—make plans to actually pull back from the battle line—whatever that takes for you. Where is your life in danger right now, and what would it look like for you to pull back in order to regroup and set new strategy in God's presence? You will need to know what to pull away *from* in order to be on retreat. Second, what kind of retreat environment will put the most distance between you and the battle line? See appendix one for more specific ideas on how to plan your retreat.

While on retreat. In the quiet of retreat time, ask yourself and do some journaling around these questions:

~ Where am I in danger these days? Say something honest to God about what you are noticing.

~ Am I engaged in the right battle(s)?

Your answers will deepen in honesty and insight as you quiet yourself in God's presence and get in touch with your own soul.

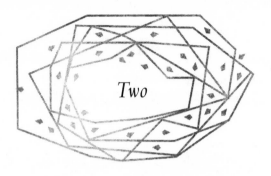

Two

JUST FLOP DOWN

We aren't rest-filled people who
occasionally become restless; we're restless
people who sometimes find rest.

HENRI NOUWEN

I REMEMBER PREPARING TO LEAD A RETREAT awhile back, and as I packed to leave I was overcome with a crushing awareness of how tired I was, how desperate I was for a fresh encounter with God, and how much I needed the realities I would be pointing others to. I could tell I was drifting into a danger zone because I actually felt *jealous* of the folks I was going to be leading into retreat—like they were going to get something I wanted—and being jealous of the people you are leading is never a good sign!

Fortunately, because I was at least somewhat practiced at paying attention to such warning signals, I knew better than to wait for a better time. I also remembered this from Emile Griffin: "When should I make a retreat? When there is no time to do it, that's when you most need to unclutter the calendar and go apart to pray. When the gridlock of your schedule forbids it. . . . That is when your heart beats against the prison walls of your enslavement and says, 'Yes, Lord, I want to spend time with you.'"

So in addition to getting ready for the retreat I was to lead, I packed another simpler bag and made arrangements for an overnight retreat *for myself* that would enable me to leave right from that engagement to enter into twenty-four hours of silent retreat for myself.

The ability to notice and name dangerous levels of exhaustion in my life, and the choice to retreat from danger in order to be replenished, brought me back from the brink of disaster. While I was leading others, I was buoyed up by the fact that I would soon be on retreat myself, free to just be a soul in God's presence. And when I emerged from my own retreat, I was able to reenter my life refreshed in body, mind, and soul, I was more grounded in God's presence in my own life, and I was no longer jealous of others who were being given the gift of a retreat!

DANGEROUSLY TIRED

There are at least two kinds of tired we might experience—good tired and dangerous tired. The differences between the two are important because the remedy for each one is different. *Good* tired is the poured out feeling we experience after a job well done or an unusually intense season of activity. Remedies for that include a good night's sleep, our normal Sabbath, a weekend off, or even a vacation. But the condition of being *dangerously* tired is not simply the result of an intense run of activity or even a crisis, as demanding as these may be. Dangerous levels of exhaustion usually accumulate over a longer period of time in which we are consistently living beyond human limits, functioning outside our giftedness, or not paying attention to the sources of our exhaustion.

When we are dangerously tired we are unable to be our best selves, we find it difficult to make wise and discerning decisions, we hoard energy rather than being able to give ourselves freely to others, and our bodies may begin to break down under the stress and strain of it all.

On a recent eight-day retreat, I described to the spiritual director who had been assigned to me the complexities of my life and the many responsibilities I juggle daily. I explained (okay, maybe I did whine a little) what I have come to identify as my five full-time lives—my full family life (my own husband, our dearly loved grown daughters and their husbands, sweet grandchildren, aging parents all living nearby), my writing commit-ments (as much as I love it, I'm always behind on something), leading retreats and speaking, leadership of the Transforming Center, and taking care of myself, which includes cultivating my own relationship with God. Count them. Five.

When we are dangerously tired we are unable to be our best selves.

In a perfect world without the limits of time and space, I would *love* to give full time to all of these blessed aspects of my life, but instead, like everyone else, I juggle. All the time. Even though I put a brave face on it most of the time, the truth is I am never quite sure if I am keeping all the balls in the air, and I always have a vague sense that I am disappointing someone. What I do know is that I try. Really hard. And it is that constant *trying* so *hard* on so many fronts all the time that often leaves me on the brink of exhaustion.

I have learned that exhaustion from juggling so many balls so much of the time is not going to be touched by shorter times spent in solitude. In fact, that is what caused me to leave the country for eight days of silence in company with the Jesuits, who know how to do silence well. It was the only way I knew to let go of all the responsibility *for a time* and drop into a deeper, quieter place in which I could rest, hear God beyond all the demands of my life, others' expectations and my own inner compulsions. It is what

brought me to this moment of sitting across from a spiritual director in a tearful heap trying to explain it all, looking for perspective, desperate for rest.

OH WHAT A RELIEF IT IS!

It did not take long for my spiritual director to snag a book off his
shelf and suggest that I read it—*When the Body Says No: Exploring
the Stress-Disease Connection* by medical doctor Gabor Mate. The
title alone was so evocative I almost felt I didn't need to read the
book! But I did read it, and one of the things that stuck with me
was this statement: "Excessive stress occurs when the demands
made on an organism exceed that organism's reasonable capacities
to fill them."

Boom. There you have it. My life in a nutshell! Worth the price of
the retreat. What followed was gentle instruction from my director
that was music to my ears. He said all I needed to do that day was to
settle down and settle in, continuing to let go of all I had left behind.
"Don't do much or work too hard at anything," he said. "Just be."

Sometimes it's good to simply follow instructions, especially this
kind of instruction. Following instructions and trusting someone
else to guide us is one aspect of resting for those of us who try so
hard. Once we have pulled away and gotten ourselves to wherever
we are going, the first invitation is always to *rest*. In fact, I've become
convinced that the optimal starting time for a retreat is in the
evening, so the first thing we do is to start letting go and dropping
some of our defenses by entering into a good night's sleep. Sleep is
a natural way to slow our pace, to lower the defenses that keep us
from being honest and receptive to God, to let go (at least a little
bit) of our attachment to life at home, and allow the inner chaos to
settle. Without this kind of rest, much of what needs to happen on
retreat will not be possible.

JUST FLOP DOWN

Catherine Doherty, Russian author and founder of the Madonna House in Ontario, has written a delightful book called *Poustinia*—the Russian word that literally means *desert*. Doherty notes that *poustinia* also refers to the "quiet lonely place that people wish to enter" in order to find the "God who dwells within them." It can refer to "truly isolated places to which specially called people go as hermits to seek God in solitude, silence and prayer for the rest of their lives," but it can also refer to a simple room in a convent or a monastery, the corner of an attic or a basement, or even a part of a room separated by a curtain. What makes the space a *poustinia* is the purpose of the person entering it—to retreat from normal life to be with God and God alone.

In her inimitable style, Catherine describes approaching the *poustinia*. "In a dazed state of mind you may be wondering: What do I do? Relax! There is nothing mysterious about it! Sometimes we are so exhausted mentally, morally, and physically that we can't do much of anything. Going into the *poustinia* we just flop down! Well, to sleep in the arms of Christ is a pretty good idea."

I cannot tell you how many times I have arrived on retreat and just flopped down! When I finished leading the retreat I mentioned earlier and finally made it to my own retreat, I remember being so tired from standing in front of people all day I could barely walk, could barely get my suitcase and pillow to my room. I was tired and hungry too, so I had to prioritize. Too tired to try to find food, somehow I got my clothes off and crawled into bed feeling my body ache, so grateful to be completely out of sight, no words required, no social interactions to manage, nothing to offer anyone, so grateful for the gift of rest that was more than just physical.

I was grateful for rest for my body. But the psychic, spiritual rest that is possible when we drop completely out of sight is what I needed even more. Knowing I would wake up the following

morning with some of the edge taken off my exhaustion and that
I would not have to use the energy that was slowly seeping back
into me to work or to manage relationships with other people was
part of the gift. Instead, I knew there was time and space to keep
sinking into the ground of my being, which is God, knowing I
would actually be able to use whatever strength and energy I had
to be present to God, which is what I most needed—and wanted.
Aware that one night of sleep was not going to fully address the
levels of exhaustion I was experiencing, it was reassuring to know
I would have time to nap the next day as needed.

If we are honest, many of us have given up hope that we will ever
be rested. We have succumbed to the belief that life is out of control
and we have no choice but to walk
through it exhausted. We're convinced
that being rested is simply not an
option or that it is a luxury only few
can afford. But God's invitation to you
on retreat is to "just flop down"—to let
your body call the shots, at least at first.

*God's invitation
to you on retreat is
to "just flop down."*

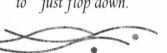

Structure your retreat so that when you need to rest you can rest in
God's presence. Let go of all the pushing and striving for productivity
that usually characterizes your life and believe that in the resting, you
are entering into Jesus' invitation to all his busy disciples.

Practicing RETREAT

Preparing for retreat. If possible, plan for your retreat in such a way that it begins with rest for your body. This might mean starting in the evening so you can pray a little bit, simply trust yourself to God, and then go to sleep. Or determining that no matter when you arrive, you will take a nap if you feel like it!

While on retreat. As you prepare for bed, especially the first night, let the act of crawling into bed and laying your head on your pillow become an exercise in trusting your whole self—body and soul—to God. As you pull the covers over yourself, imagine that God is putting his arms around you, holding you, covering you with his love. Feel the tiredness in your body and enjoy how good it feels to lie there, invited by God to relax and rest. If cares and concerns surface, trust these to God even as you trust yourself to God. If you wake up in the night (which often happens on the first night in a strange place), don't fight your wakefulness; just allow yourself to become aware that you are with God and God is with you, looking on you with love as you rest. In this way, you are still resting your soul even as your body is awake.

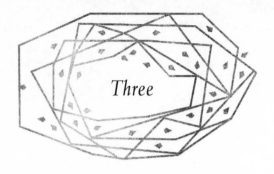

Three

The SOURCES *of* OUR EXHAUSTION

Because we do not rest, we lose our way.

Wayne Muller

❦ ❦ ❦

IT IS IMPOSSIBLE TO OVERSTATE the level of exhaustion many of us are experiencing these days and how dangerous it is. Christian busyness layered on top of the stresses of life in our culture, along with the more subtle sources of exhaustion that are harder to identify, means we are all at risk of drifting into dangerous levels of exhaustion before we even know it!

There are reasons why we end up as tired as we are, and one of the keys to being able to enter into retreat in a restorative way is to note the sources of our exhaustion so we can rest *at the source*. I've already noted two sources of exhaustion that plague most, if not all, of us—the exhaustion that comes from always being plugged in and available, and the exhaustion that comes from trying so hard and juggling so much. But other *more subtle* sources of exhaustion plague serious

Christians these days, and it is important that we become aware of them. Then, rather than exhausting ourselves further by trying to figure out how to fix it on our own, on retreat we can ask God, "What are we going to do about *that*?" and listen for what God has to say.

WHY ARE WE SO TIRED?

The following are some common sources of our exhaustion.

We are functioning out of an inordinate sense of ought and should. As Christians, or simply as responsible human beings, many of us feel that we should be willing to be exhausted in the service of God and others, and that this is normal. We have unreasonable expectations that we should be a never-ending fountain of love, goodwill, and service at all times and in all places. We don't know how to live with our humanness, and we feel guilty or at least uncomfortable with ourselves when we are ill, tired, grieving, or confused. Not knowing what to do with these human aspects of ourselves, we try to shove them down and keep them under the surface or just outside our awareness. But even that takes energy; shoving them down creates a slow leak, draining us of our energy over time. In the process, unhealed emotion and exhaustion gets buried alive. But make no mistake—it is all still there and these buried dynamics will eventually make themselves known in uglier and more destructive ways than if we had simply acknowledged them and dealt with them honestly and openly.

We find it difficult or even humiliating to receive help from others. Remember the apostle Peter, who found it so difficult to let Jesus wash his feet even though he had seen Jesus allow Mary to wash Jesus' own feet the previous week? What is really going on there? This resistance to allowing others to serve us is often rooted in our perception of ourselves as servants of others—including Jesus—and this is the identity we are most comfortable with. Those of us who have been following Jesus for a long time are always asking him,

"What can I do for you?" And we assume that Jesus always wants us to do more because there is always more to do.

We might also notice that serving others is one way of maintaining control of our interactions with others, keeping us in the one-up position. Here is a way to observe how you really feel about serving and being served. Have you ever participated in a foot-washing at a church service, perhaps during Holy Week? Maybe you knew this was coming (so you were somewhat prepared), or maybe you were caught off guard, but the question is, which role were you most uncomfortable with: being the person whose feet were washed, or being the one doing the washing? Most of us would rather wash someone else's feet than have our own feet washed. Allowing someone to serve us in this way puts them in touch with a very human and maybe even less-than-perfect aspect of ourselves (our feet!); it puts them in control of the interaction, which is uncomfortable, to say the least!

We might be living more as a performer than as the person God created us to be. Functioning out of *oughts* and *shoulds* results in a performance mentality in which we become increasingly disconnected from our authentic self. We might even develop a subtle conviction that we are valuable only when we are performing. The simplest way to understand this is that *oughts* and *shoulds* come from someone else, so when we are doing things because we think we should, we are reacting and responding to something outside ourselves. Authentic desire, on the other hand, comes from within and is a part of who we are.

Authentic desire comes from within and is a part of who we are.

A wise spiritual person always listens and pays attention to the subtle distinction between *oughts* and *shoulds* and the authentic desires God has placed within them. It takes more energy to *perform* than to *be* the person God created us to be. Perhaps you have already noticed that when you are functioning out of your essential, created self, you can actually accomplish a lot without being overly tired. But when you are performing, even the smallest tasks can wear you out.

When our sense of self-worth is derived from our performance, it is difficult to stop performing. In fact, performing in order to gain the approval of others or to maintain a sense of self can become a compulsion; we may feel we will cease to exist if we disconnect from this perceived source of identity and self-worth. A good question to promote self-awareness regarding this dynamic is to ask, When was the last time I let someone help me or serve me in a way that put me in a vulnerable position? What was that like? (Remember, we're not trying to fix anything yet; we are just trying to notice.)

We may have few, or no, boundaries on our service and availability to others. We always feel we should do more because there is always more to do. The result can be a nonstop pace of life that, at its best, is tied to genuine passion for what we do, genuine longing to experience life fully, to go through every open door, to seize every opportunity, and to contribute to every good cause and mission. But we can also reach a point where our genuine gifts and passions wear us out because it's so exciting we don't know when to stop. We can become addicted to the adrenaline this excitement produces, or to the sense of importance we gain from it, but eventually we crash against the wall of human limitation.

Psychologists would call this tendency toward lack of boundaries and constant availability "poor emotional differentiation." Differentiation describes the differences that exist among people and the ability we have to experience ourselves as complete and emotionally separate from the systems we are a part of, while also staying connected. The more differentiated we are, the more we are able to operate from a thoughtful inner guidance system rather than being held hostage by the emotions and expectations of others. We know where we end and the other person begins; we are able to operate from our deepest values rather than being sucked in by others' priorities for us and the emotions that surround those priorities. We are able to calm our own emotional responses enough to make decisions based on our own internal values and goals (basic or solid self).

This seems to be what Jesus was trying to convey to his disciples in Mark 6. In the midst of their excitement about their first ministry excursion, his invitation to "Come away . . . and rest a while" was not a form of punishment because they had been doing something wrong. The disciples had been doing everything right. They had been doing exactly what Jesus told them to in the power he had given them, and the results were exciting. Addicting, even!

By calling them to "come away and rest a while" in the midst of so much human need, Jesus was getting on the prevention side of this human tendency. He was guiding them into a healthy and sustainable lifestyle by helping them establish boundaries and rhythms around their availability to others. He did not want them to wear themselves out to the point where they would be no good to anyone.

We are carrying the great burden of unhealed wounds—sadness, unresolved tension, toxicity in one or more of our relationships. Many of us have never been taught how to grieve our hurts and losses, what to do with unresolved tension, how to identify and extricate ourselves from toxic relationships, or how to shift unhealthy patterns. Some of us aren't even sure we're allowed to do this, and so we soldier on, trying to manage it all and keep it under wraps. We think we can handle it. We've been told that a good Christian *should be able to handle it*. But the truth is that our effort to manage all that is unresolved within us is draining our life energy.

Our effort to manage all that is unresolved within us is draining our life energy.

The practice of retreat provides the needed time and space to be with the difficult, hurting places of our lives—not for problem solving or fixing (because not everything can be fixed) but to stop holding it in so bravely. It provides the context in which we can release emotion, let go a little bit (or a lot) in God's presence, and allow God to comfort us as only God can. When we don't have regular time and space for allowing God access for attending to the wounds of our lives, we get weary from holding it in, and eventually we will begin to disintegrate.

We may be experiencing information overload. There is no end to the amount of information available to us, but there is a limit to how much time and energy we can expend on taking it in and processing it. Some personality types are more prone than others to getting caught up in the constant flow of information and even binging on it without knowing it! Our minds are exhausted from trying to gather and make sense of all the information coming at us, and our hearts are exhausted from the emotion that is stirred up by the complexity and the heart-break of what is going on in our world. At some point we simply have to take a break from it all; we have to recognize this as a source of our exhaustion and take a rest from it. To stay on a Spirit-guided path, we need to ask, Am I going to keep gathering information, or am I going to take the next step on my spiritual journey?

We may be mired in our own willfulness. Willfulness describes *our attempts to impose our own ideas on others, establish our own agenda, and control everything around us.* It might manifest itself in our determined efforts to force something into reality that just isn't happening—on a spiritual level, at least—and a refusal to accept reality as it is. For whatever reason, something we want is not being given to us, at least not right now, but we keep pushing for it anyway. Or we refuse to ac-knowledge or accept something that *is* happening.

This refusal to *accept what is* means we are constantly using energy to fight reality in favor of a reality that exists only in our own mind.

The result of this willful lack of acceptance is that we hold ourselves back from what actually is happening, separating ourselves and resisting what *is* rather than giving ourselves to the gift of now. It's sort of like a tired, grumpy child who resists naptime. The gift of *now* is the nap offered to us by a parent who is wise and generous and knows what's best. When the gift contained in the *now* (a nap) is refused, not only does the child expend needless energy resisting and getting all worked up, the remainder of the day is harder on everyone—including the child. On the other hand, if the child says yes to what is actually happening in the current moment, everything goes better!

Willfulness can be a manifestation of narcissism in which spiritual methods, practices, and ideas are used to promote our own agenda. When we are willful we use God talk to convince ourselves (and others) that we are "doing God's will," when in fact we are simply insisting on our own way. There is also the kind of willfulness that manifests itself in using our energy to run from God—as Jonah and the Israelites did—rather than going with what God is doing. This kind of running and resisting is exhausting.

On retreat we may be able to acknowledge willfulness as a source of our exhaustion and notice all the ways it is wearing us down. As God reveals this to us, we may then be ready to enter into the opposite of willfulness, which is *willingness*—the willingness to accept and to enter into what *is* happening spiritually. The willingness to accept that someone else's wisdom may be better than our own.

As I have come more in touch with my own willfulness, I have been helped by this breath prayer from Richard Rohr: *God, humble me in the presence of reality.* This prayer has changed my life generally and has changed my responses to specific moments (when I have remembered to pray it). It has helped me release the death grip I have on life and people and situations so I can "rest into" what is and accept it as God's will and plan for me on this day. This prayer is humbling because it leads me to trust God—with my life and my destiny, with situations and their outcomes, with people and their choices—at times when I might have worn myself out fighting realities that are not mine to fight or control.

In the safety of a retreat environment, we can ask ourselves, Where in my life am I willfully resisting reality in favor of an ideal that exists in my own mind? What would it look like and feel like to choose *willingness* instead? If you would like more guidance on moving beyond willfulness to willingness, the best resource I know of is *Will and Spirit* by Gerald May.

WHEN GOD WAITS FOR US

Isaiah 30 contains a chilling portrait of a willful people who look a lot like us—people who "carry out a plan, but not mine," God says,

> who set out to go down to Egypt
>> without asking for my counsel,
> to take refuge in the protection of Pharaoh
>> and to seek shelter in the shadow of Egypt. (v. 2)

To support themselves in their willful choices so as not to be challenged, they

> say to the seers, "Do not see";
>> and to the prophets, "Do not prophesy to us what is right;
> speak to us smooth things,
>> prophesy illusions,
> leave the way, turn aside from the path,
>> let us hear no more about the Holy One of Israel."
>> (vv. 10-11)

Rather than trusting God for their basic needs and saying yes to his invitations, they are a willful people returning to the place of their former bondage, looking to old sources for safety, security, and survival.

In the midst of all that seduction, God makes this counterintuitive statement: "In returning and rest you shall be saved; / in quietness and trust shall be your strength." But still they run the other way, refusing God's rest—refusing the only solution to all they are facing. So what does God do? God does the only thing he can do: God waits. For them and for us. *Therefore the LORD waits to be gracious to you; / therefore he will rise up to show mercy to you.*

Practicing retreat is one way to turn from our willfulness and say yes to God's invitation to rest—an invitation that is always there for us. It is an opportunity to rest, not just physically but also to attend to the *sources* of our exhaustion, allowing God to lead us into the kind of rest that corresponds specifically to those sources. Thomas Merton asserts,

> Some of us need to discover that we will not begin to live more fully until we have the courage to do and see and taste and experience much less than usual. . . . There are times when in order to keep ourselves in existence at all we simply have to sit back for a while and do nothing. And for a man who has let himself be drawn completely out of himself by his activity, nothing is more difficult than to sit still and rest, doing nothing at all. The very act of resting is the hardest and most courageous act he can perform.

Retreat as a spiritual practice is not a vacation; it is not a day at the spa or on the golf course. It is coming home to ourselves in God's presence and resting there. God is waiting for us, continuing to hold out to us the invitation to rest. The only question is, will we say yes or will we keep running the other way?

Practicing retreat is one way to turn from our willfulness and say yes to God's invitation to rest.

Practicing RETREAT

Preparing for retreat or while on retreat. With the Holy Spirit as your guide, prayerfully review the sources of exhaustion described in this chapter.

~ functioning out of an inordinate sense of *ought* and *should*

~ finding it difficult or even humiliating to receive help from others

~ living more as a performer than the person God created me to be

~ few or no boundaries on my service and availability to others

~ always feeling I should be doing more because there is always more to do

~ carrying the burden of unhealed wounds—sadness, unresolved tension, toxicity in relationships

~ information overload

~ my own willfulness

Which resonate most deeply with you?

Take time to journal about what you are seeing and knowing. How can you structure your retreat time or enter into and engage in retreat time in such a way that you can rest at the source(s) of your exhaustion?

You too may need a spiritual director or a spiritual friend to help you get in touch with the sources of your exhaustion and to support you in seeking *God's wisdom* for attending to these sources.

INTERLUDE

How shall my heart be reconciled to its feast of losses?

STANLEY KUNITZ

The Knapsack

I am not good at grieving my losses
and moving on.
I carry them in a knapsack
hanging heavy on my chest.
Doesn't everyone see me stoop beneath the weight?

Don't you ever get to put it down? someone asks.
No, I reply, *it is with me always,*
more present on most days than God himself.

Grief gets added every day,
or so it seems.
Oh, it's o.k., I say.
It's just one more grief to tuck into my knapsack.
I've learned how to walk
with heaviness around my neck.
I know how to enter rooms
back straight
smile bright
as though nothing was hanging there.

But today I am tired.
The weight of accumulated grief
is more than I can carry.

Where does one go to unpack grief?
To take out each loss
and hold it in your hand
To wonder where it goes
and then put it in its place?

I don't cry about my grief anymore,
although there are always tears
behind my eyes.
The tears are stuck inside now—
Like stones in a graveyard
they have settled heavy
into the landscape of my life

I've heard that depression is the refusal to mourn.
I don't know how to mourn in a way that helps.
I don't know how.

God, if you would show me—I would do it.
If you would take me to a place
where I could truly mourn,
I would walk in—I think.
I would walk into that graveyard
And lay myself down on the grave
of each and every dead thing
and let my tears fall into the earth.

And then I would get up
And walk out into my life.

Ruth Haley Barton, 2008

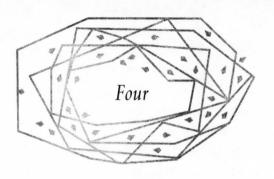

Four

FINDING YOUR RHYTHM *on* RETREAT

We are blessed with these inner rhythms that
tell us where we are, and where we are going. No matter,
then, our fifty- and sixty-hour work weeks, the refusing to stop
for lunch, the bypassing sleep and working deep into the darkness.
If we stop, if we return to rest, our natural state asserts itself.
Our natural wisdom and balance come to our aid, and we
can find our way to what is good, necessary, and true.

WAYNE MULLER

HUMAN BEINGS ARE MADE *with* rhythms and *for* rhythms. The rhythms of our breathing, heart rate, and brain waves keep us alive, and nature itself has a pulse that orders all of life. Whether it's the circadian rhythms of sleeping and waking; eating three times a day; working and resting; the seasonal rhythms of winter, spring, summer, and fall; the undulating rhythm of the tides; or the life-sustaining rhythms of our breathing, heartbeat, and brain waves—human beings thrive within rhythms. In fact, if they are healthy all organisms follow life-sustaining rhythms, and if it were not for these rhythms we would all be lost in chaos and confusion.

Retreat is an amazing opportunity to return to our natural rhythms and discover (or rediscover) what is good and necessary and true at the core of our lives. It will be important for you to find *your* own rhythm on retreat as you discover (or rediscover) that which is good and necessary and true *for you*. To go to bed when you are tired—even if it's eight in the evening. To sleep until you're not tired anymore, and to have some sense of how much sleep you need. To pay attention while you eat, to take pleasure in it, and to discover what is truly needed. To sit in silence for as long as you want so the sediment in your soul starts to settle.

Human beings are made with rhythms and for rhythms.

A WELCOME CHANGE OF PACE

On retreat we have the opportunity to literally *change our pace* by entering into different rhythms designed for the special purpose of being with God and God alone. Such rhythms might be built around the rhythms of the community providing the retreat, or they can be rhythms we put in place ourselves, perhaps with the help of a spiritual director. They can be as fully orbed as those of a monastic community that practices fixed-hour prayers throughout the day, or it could be as simple as celebrating the Eucharist every day, participating with others in centering prayer at an appointed time, or seeing a spiritual director once a day and following the guidance you receive.

Of course there will be the basic rhythms of eating and sleeping, and it is good to balance those with engaging your body in physical work or exercise. Mealtimes can provide some structure as you incorporate simple mealtime prayers and allow yourself to be more attentive to the experience of savoring your food and receiving it with gratitude.

Within more restful rhythms we start to slow down—to walk without rushing, eat without gulping, and pray without looking at our watches. Retreat rhythms should also allow for as much rest as we need—especially early on—rather than creating too rigorous a schedule. Ordering your retreat time around a rhythm of fixed-hour prayers, which would naturally include Scripture reading and time for reflection, can provide a skeleton schedule within which everything else will pretty much fall into place.

Even if you don't put a lot into planning your rhythms ahead of time, you may discover that rhythms emerge quite naturally just because that's the way we have been created.

KEEPING THE MAIN THING THE MAIN THING

I have done retreats many different ways—everything from going somewhere that provides no structure at all (a hermitage for total solitude, a simple bed and breakfast, a retreat center that does not have a praying community attached to it) to going to a monastery where there are multiple fixed-hour prayer services throughout the day. (I will say more about the practice of fixed-hour prayer in chapter five.) There is also such a thing as a *preached retreat*, which includes prayer plus teaching and guidance on a chosen topic woven throughout an overall atmosphere of solitude, silence, and presence to God—which is most similar to the retreats we offer in the Transforming Center.

No matter what the structure, to be a *spiritual* retreat the emphasis must remain on the primary purpose for retreat time—solitude, silence, rest, listening and responding to the Spirit of God deep within. Even in a preached retreat, where the community gathers for prayer and teaching, typically meals are taken in silence, and silence is observed throughout the retreat house. This enables participants to remain attentive to what God is doing and saying deep within, rather than being drawn out to interact with others.

Silence at meals and "in the house" is important because interactions with others kicks up all sorts of inner dynamics that are not particularly helpful for the purposes of retreat—performance anxiety, concern for how others are perceiving us, a focus on attending to others' needs, even simple curiosity—dynamics that in other settings would be perfectly normal but are a distraction from a retreat. Sometimes we don't realize how exhausted we are in the social aspects of our existence until we attend a silent retreat.

Sometimes we don't realize how exhausted we are until we attend a silent retreat.

I remember attending one "retreat" where too much was required of us way too soon. I was longing to sink into the anonymity of retreat time and had, in fact, chosen a setting where I wouldn't know anyone. However, instead of being invited into silence at the beginning of the retreat, we were asked to share our names and identifying details. Then, because silence was not held immediately following this sharing, we were left open to others' attempts to connect with us based on what had been shared. Being asked to use words, to be present to others' words, and then being approached socially that early in a retreat experience felt like an assault in my depleted state. At that point, the longing for solitude and silence was a desperate hunger I would have done anything to meet—including running out of the room before anyone could approach me.

SURPRISED BY GOD

Although the specifics of our retreat rhythms and how God meets us in them will look different for all of us, the whole point is to be able to settle into a restful way of being that leaves all sorts of ways for God to surprise us. I have been surprised by God too many times to mention, but here's what happened for me toward the end of the eight-day retreat I described in chapter two. The main rhythm of this particular retreat was celebrating the Eucharist every day just before lunch. The service lasted about forty-five minutes and took place in a lovely chapel in the round. Retreatants remained in silence, except for participating in the Scripture readings, responsive prayers, and passing of the peace in the liturgy surrounding the Eucharist. The service followed the lectionary for the Scripture readings, and every day there was a different celebrant and homilist from the Jesuit community who worked and worshiped in and around the retreat house.

About five days into it, when my soul had gotten particularly quiet, the lectionary Gospel reading at the midday Eucharist service was Matthew 16:24-28, in which Jesus offers his paradoxical teaching that those who want to save their lives must lose them. He concludes with the rhetorical question, "What will it profit [a person] if they gain the whole world but forfeit their life? Or what will they give in return for their life?" This is a passage I have spent a lot of time in, and it is very important to me. So the fact that this was one of the lectionary Gospel readings *during my retreat* struck me as significant; I was eager to hear what God might have to say.

The homilist that day was a young staff member who was still in formation as a Jesuit priest. His youthful good looks and athleticism were not exactly what I was accustomed to seeing in Jesuit retreat houses, so I was intrigued. After reading the Gospel from Matthew, he began telling us about an experience he had in the first phase of his Jesuit formation. Jesuit novices, he told us, participate in a number of different assignments—or what St. Ignatius called experiments. One of his early experiments took place at a L'Arche community composed of adults with special needs—mental and often physical disabilities—who chose to live together. Assistants also lived and participated in these communities to help with daily activities that individuals might not be able to perform on their own; in the case of those with physical disabilities, assistants would also bathe, change, and help feed them.

Kevin (the young Jesuit) was assigned to be Leonel's primary caregiver. With a great desire "to be the best Jesuit ever" and prove to his novice director how capable he was, he jumped into this opportunity with high hopes and youthful determination. He told us:

Leonel is a thirty-four-year-old man who can't speak or feed or bathe himself, and is confined to a wheelchair. In his frustration to express himself and to connect with others, he often hit himself in the face. It was very difficult spending the day with him. I often struggled to find hope in what seemed to me to be a very lonely life. Every day presented new challenges for both of us. I would go crazy (as would Leonel) trying to communicate in my broken French as he would scream out of total frustration and hit himself; I would struggle to bathe and feed him in a way he liked, and he would scream and hit himself. Long story short, we both grew increasingly impatient with each other as we searched to find what the other wanted or was trying to say.

I remember one morning, as I was giving Leonel his bath, I managed to nick his chin while shaving. By that point in the bath routine, as per usual, I was soaking wet from being repeatedly splashed, was standing in a small pool of water that had formed on the floor, and Leonel was screaming and had moved from hitting himself to trying to hit me (with absolute just cause). This was a soul-searching moment for both of us. The

only added feature this particular morning was the hemor-
rhaging of blood from Leonel's chin. . . .

In the midst of all this, there was a knock at the door and the
community leader, a lovely woman named Annette—who had
lived in L'Arche for over thirty years—came in, and observing
the water, the tears, the blood, asked, "Is everything okay?" I
turned to Leonel, who had a very familiar look on his face that
seemed to say, "Get him the $%^& out of here!" but, wanting to
be the perfect Jesuit, I said, "Absolutely—everything is fine!"

Annette, however, suggested I take a break and she would
finish things up.

After sufficient recovery time, Annette came and sat with me
and said, "You know, as much as you may want to, you can't fix
Leonel. God made him the way he is for a reason." And in her
wisdom, she added, "It may be to help people like you and me."

COMING UNDONE

As soon as Kevin started sharing his story, I could feel the tears start
to come, but, not wanting to draw attention to myself, I struggled
mightily to hold back or at least hide them. By the time Kevin got to
the point where Annette said, "You know, as much as you may want
to, you can't fix Leonel," I was openly weeping, and others were as well.
We were undone.

Somehow the picture of this strong and capable priest wrestling
with a disabled young man, trying his Jesuit best to offer help to another human being but being completely bested by the whole situation, broke me open. I had no idea what was happening except that
this image, so compellingly drawn, seemed to capture some sort of
essential truth about my whole life and its striving. In his story, I was
seeing something about myself that I had not seen nearly as clearly
before—all the places in my life that I tried so hard to fix what couldn't
be fixed, and yet I kept trying.

I did not want to accept Annette's statement that "as much as you may want to, you can't fix Leonel. God made him that way for a reason," and yet God brought Jesus' statement in John 9 straight into my weary, broken, hard-working heart to corroborate its truth: This man "was born blind so that God's works might be revealed in him." I couldn't escape it—what Jesus seems to be saying is that at some point, all of our fixing and trying to figure things out actually works against the purposes of God in a given situation. At some point, in order for the job to get done, we must let go and wait for God to take over and finish things up—otherwise, we just get in the way. I was suddenly aware of at least two areas in my life where I knew I had been working overtime trying to fix something that couldn't be fixed, and there was blood, sweat, and tears all over the floor. In case anyone was asking, I just kept saying everything was fine but Jesus was saying, "Why don't you take a break and let me finish up here?"

RHYTHMS THAT CREATE SPACE FOR GOD

Kevin brought his story full circle with the Gospel reading by stating that perhaps giving up our efforts to fix things in our own strength and through our own ideas about how things should be done is one way we are called to lose our lives in order to find them. He offered this perspective from Henri Nouwen: "Our life is full of brokenness—broken relationships, broken promises, broken expectations. How can we live with that brokenness without becoming bitter and resentful except by returning again and again to God's faithful presence in our lives?"

And that was my one final humbling: I had to admit that, yes, I had become

> *Perhaps giving up our efforts to fix things in our own strength and through our own ideas about how things should be done is one way we are called to lose our lives in order to find them.*

bitter and resentful regarding those places where all my attempts at fixing weren't working—blaming my bitterness on those who didn't seem to be on board with what my attempts at fixing entailed. I had allowed bitterness and resentment to take up residence in my heart so as to avoid facing my own willfulness and impotence in the face of matters that were outside my ability to control. Lord have mercy. How do we get ourselves tied up in spiritual knots like this?

Rhythms help us rest, they hold us and carry us through retreat time, and they create space for so many opportunities to be surprised by God.

Without the community's rhythm of sharing the Eucharist every day along with Scripture readings, prayers, and reflections—coupled with my own willingness to give myself to it—I'm not sure God could have penetrated my heart and my defenses in quite the same way. Being "alone together" was part of what God used so powerfully on this retreat.

Having rhythms in place while on retreat—whether provided by the community or created for ourselves—opens up space for God to do something surprising, something we could not have orchestrated for ourselves. Rhythms help us rest, they hold us and carry us through retreat time, and they create space for so many opportunities to be surprised by God.

Practicing RETREAT

Preparing for retreat, or early in your retreat time. Don't overplan your retreat but instead allow yourself the lovely freedom to settle into your body and soul, and enter into rhythms that are good for you.

If you are entering a community that already has some sort of a schedule for meals, prayer times, and communal experiences, start with that and work with it. Then pay attention to your bodily rhythms of sleep and eating.

Go to bed when you're tired. Sleep until you wake up. Find out what your body cries out for when it has the opportunity.

Make sure to get some physical activity or exercise: take a run in the morning before breakfast, go for a walk after lunch or dinner. You might also want to schedule time after breakfast for spiritual reading and a nap sometime in the afternoon.

If you are receiving spiritual direction, take a few minutes before your appointment to discern what you would like to bring to that conversation. After the appointment, make sure you give yourself time to capture what seems most important from that session in your journal, or to pray and talk with God about it. If you are making your own schedule, add prayer times in ways that fit with other aspects of the schedule the retreat house has in place.

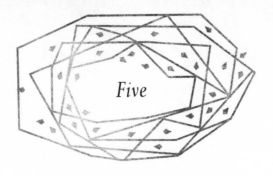

SWEET HOURS
of PRAYER

When we go on retreat, we clear space for God's action
in our calendar. . . . Making a retreat requires a certain
kind of trust. . . . We don't know what God has in store for
us, but we are willing to risk what we will find out.

EMILE GRIFFIN

＊　♦　＊

THE FIRST TIME I ENTERED INTO rhythms of fixed-hour prayer
while on retreat, I felt like I had come home to a place I had never
been and yet a place in which I truly belonged. It was a simple evening
prayer service signaling the beginning of a spiritual retreat with a few
like-minded souls. One of the persons in our group had experience
with fixed-hour prayer and prepared a simple liturgy using prayers
from the Psalms, a reading from the Gospels, and written prayers from
the Book of Common Prayer and the Methodist hymnal. We set aside
a simple prayer space. We entered that space in silence. We lit a candle

to signify Christ's presence with us through the Holy Spirit. And then we prayed the prayers provided for us:

> From the rising of the sun to its setting,
> Let the name of the Lord be praised.
> YOU, O LORD, ARE MY LAMP.
> MY GOD, YOU MAKE MY DARKNESS BRIGHT.
> Light and peace in Jesus Christ our Lord.
> THANKS BE TO GOD.

Some of the prayers were read in unison; some were read responsively—and I just lost myself in the beauty and simplicity of it all. Instead of having to work hard to think up some words to pray, I simply gave myself to the beauty of words that expressed deep longings and powerful praises that were true in me but I could never have found the words to say. Instead of getting caught up in my ego's attempts to say something profound to God (and to the people around me), I rested from all of that and *prayed*. Instead of listening to someone else's interpretation or application of Scripture, I heard Scripture read without comment and listened for what God was saying to me in the context of our relationship. Instead of having to endure an exhausting round of overly stimulating programming, this small group of us settled into a silence so rich and satisfying that I lost all track of time until someone finally nudged me to remind me that it was my turn to read Scripture!

That was fifteen years ago, and that little group of likeminded souls became the Transforming Center, and we have been praying this way ever since!

Today in every one of our retreats we gather eight times for short, fifteen-to-twenty-minute prayer services, beginning with evening and night prayers on the first night, morning, midday, evening, and night prayers on the second day, and morning and midday prayer/leaving service on the third day. This is, quite simply, what we do. Many who have joined us over the years cite the practice of fixed-hour prayer in community as one of the most precious spiritual opportunities of retreat time. Praying the great prayers of the church, listening to Scripture, holding some silence together, and joining our voices in simple, worshipful songs grounds us in spiritual reality and creates space for God to speak clearly to our souls. The rhythm of fixed-hour prayer literally shapes our souls—alone and together.

RHYTHMS THAT GIVE SHAPE TO OUR DESIRE

One of the best things about going on retreat is the opportunity to enter into different rhythms than we typically experience in normal life, or at least not to the same extent. Even though I am a flaming P (perceiving) on the Meyers-Briggs Type Indicator—which means that

One of the best things about going on retreat is the opportunity to enter into different rhythms than we typically experience in normal life.

I prefer a spontaneous, open-ended, unstructured existence—I find that a little bit of structure actually helps me rest because then I'm not faced with decisions every minute about what to do; rhythms *give shape and structure* to my desire and intention to seek God.

As our souls are quieted in the silence and receptivity of retreat, rhythms of prayer, receiving the daily Eucharist, hearing Scriptures read, or meeting with a spiritual director are more effective than usual because the surface chop of our emotions is settling down, making us more receptive to whatever word of love, wisdom, or challenge God has for us; somehow, whatever is given penetrates more deeply. Just like a rock thrown into the calm surface of a pond creates ripples all the way out to the edges, as our souls settle down the gifts of God can be received more deeply, touching every aspect of our lives.

During such times it is not unusual to be caught off guard by the welling up of tears, a sense of being in the presence of the holy or an experience of being penetrated by truth; we may not even know why something affects us so deeply until we have time to reflect on it. And the spacious rhythms of retreat ensure that we have just that—time and space to actually *be with* whatever is happening within us—staying with it long enough to plumb whatever depths need to be plumbed. It's not that we don't have similar experiences of God in the midst of normal life, but we usually have to rush off to the next thing and there is no time to pay attention.

PRAYING LIKE JESUS PRAYED

If you are not familiar with fixed-hour prayer, it is a Christian practice rooted in Jewish tradition and in the patterns of the early church. Indeed, it is one of the oldest ways of praying—so old, in fact, that it is not even taught overtly in Scripture, it is merely assumed. In his book *Praying with the Church*, Scot McKnight points out that it would have been nearly impossible for Jesus and his disciples to be practicing Jews in the first century without participating in Jewish rhythms of prayer. In fact, the Psalms *were* the Hebrew prayer book, and practicing Jews prayed from the Psalms daily, providing them an opportunity to constantly recite those biblical passages central to their spirituality.

David alludes to the practice of fixed-hour prayer in Psalm 55 when he says,

I call upon God. . . .
Evening, morning and at noon
    I utter my complaint and moan,
    and he will hear my voice.

Daniel prayed three times a day in spite of the threat to his life if he did so. Peter received his vision regarding Cornelius while he was saying midday prayers. And in Acts 3, the first healing miracle after the ascension took place as Peter and John were on their way to

3 p.m. prayers in the temple. So whenever we pray from the Psalms, we are using the same prayer book as Jesus and his disciples!

Fixed-hour prayer is a powerful practice because the prayers themselves contain a combination of some or all the following elements: an opening or an invocation that invites God's presence, a psalm or a prayer taken directly from the Psalms, a Scripture reading, the Lord's prayer, a creed that gives us the opportunity to affirm our faith, a Collect or some other prayer of the church that gathers up our shared intent, a time for silent reflection, perhaps a hymn, and a benediction or a parting blessing. In many cases, these elements are nuanced to help us turn our hearts toward God in the specific context of the hour being prayed—lauds (morning), midday, vespers (evening), compline (prayer before retiring). They are the spiritual equivalent of a vitamin-packed power drink!

Fixed-hour prayer is one of the oldest ways of praying.

Becoming familiar with these fixed hours can orient you to the community's prayer times or can help you set up your own. Although most monastic communities pray seven times a day, I suggest the following basic four (or even just two—morning and night) as a way to get started.

Morning prayer (lauds). In the morning, we can begin with praise, affirming God's presence with us, receiving his loving care toward us and committing the day to him. (If you are praying with others, the upper- and lowercase lines are for the leader, and the all uppercase lines are for everyone to read together. If you are praying alone, you will read/pray all the words.)

O GOD, OPEN OUR LIPS AND WE SHALL DECLARE YOUR PRAISE.

God said: Let there be light; and there was light.

And God saw that the light was good. This very day the Lord
has acted!

LET US REJOICE!

Praise the Lord!

GOD'S NAME BE PRAISED!

Midday prayer. At midday, when we might be starting to get a
little bored or lose our focus—maybe we are even tempted to seek a
distraction or stimulation of some sort—we stop to refocus on our
spiritual desire, renew our intention, and return to a place of rest in
him for a few moments. This simple opening prayer might be our
heart cry:

O God, make speed to save us.

O Lord, make haste to help us.

Often midday prayer will contain some sort of a prayer for wisdom,
such as this Collect for grace, which is one of my favorites.

O God, by whom we are guided in judgment, and who raises up
for us light in the darkness, grant us, in all our doubts and un-
certainties, the grace to ask what you would have us to do; that
your spirit of wisdom may save us from all false choices, and in
your straight path we may not stumble;

Through Jesus Christ our Lord. AMEN.

Especially if we have brought a question for discernment into our
retreat time, this prayer can be tremendously grounding, bring us back
to our deepest intent, and help us return to a listening stance.

Evening prayer (vespers). As the sun sets and the natural light
fades, we acknowledge God as the source of our light and greet one
other with expressions of peace.

YOU, O LORD, ARE MY LAMP,

MY GOD YOU MAKE MY DARKNESS BRIGHT.

Light and in Jesus Christ our Lord,

THANKS BE TO GOD!

In many communities, evening prayer is the longest of the prayer services, offering us the opportunity to place the cares of the day in God's hand as we make the transition from daytime to the evening hours.

We praise you and thank you, O God,

FOR YOU ARE WITHOUT BEGINNING AND WITHOUT END.

Through Christ, you created the whole world;

THROUGH CHRIST, PRESERVE IT.

Through Christ you made the day for the works of light

AND THE NIGHT FOR THE REFRESHMENT OF OUR MINDS AND OUR BODIES.

Keep us now in Christ, grant us a peaceful evening,

A NIGHT FREE FROM SIN, AND BRING US AT LAST TO ETERNAL LIFE.

Through Christ and in the Holy Spirit,

WE OFFER YOU ALL GLORY, HONOR, AND WORSHIP,

Now and forever. AMEN.

Evening prayer typically includes the Gospel reading for the day and may include a brief reflection or homily. A time of intercession for the needs of others helps keep our focus from becoming too inward, and bringing our own specific needs and burdens before the Lord helps us to keep trusting God with all we have left behind.

Written intercessions relieve us of the need to be so wordy or to expend energy trying to put things into words—a helpful discipline, given the fact this is another place where human striving and fixing can so easily take over. On retreat, our personal resting in God and "being with what is" can foster a greater capacity to hold others and their needs quietly in God's presence as well.

If we are privileged to pray in community while on retreat, written intercessions (also called "prayers of the people" in some settings) give us a way to join together in lifting up our shared concerns to God—with just a name or a phrase—and then to agree together by praying in unison,

Lord in your mercy.

HEAR OUR PRAYER.

Even if those present are strangers to one another, participating in this kind of intercessory prayer practice can be a meaningful communal experience even in the midst of our solitude.

Night prayer (compline). *Compline* means "complete," and this is how we might want to end our days on retreat as we prepare for bed— by praying a prayer that brings a sense of completion to the day. This is an opportunity for celebrating the ways we experienced God's presence with us during the day and asking him to grant us the rest we need.

May God grant us a quiet night and peace at the last.

AMEN.

It is good to give thanks to the Lord,

TO SING PRAISE TO YOUR NAME, O MOST HIGH;

To herald your love in the morning.

YOUR TRUTH AT THE CLOSE OF THE DAY.

Night prayer might also include a time of silent reflection for the *examen*, in which we notice where God was with us during the day, where God seemed absent, what invitations there were, and how we responded. We might also notice places where we have fallen short of Christlikeness, in this particular day or in general, so we can confess our sins and receive God's forgiveness. This is an important aspect of letting go of this day and calling it good, receiving God's gift of rest, and preparing to receive the new mercies that God will have prepared for us when we awaken.

RESTING IN PRAYER

One of the great blessings of entering into fixed-hour prayer and other rhythms on retreat is that it helps us rest. Since there is a schedule set for us and the prayers are written and provided, there is nothing for us to figure out. If we are using Scriptures from a common lectionary (another practice I highly recommend), we are also relieved of the need to figure out what Scriptures to read, and yet we are giving God ample opportunity to address us directly through his Word throughout our retreat time. The Gospel readings in particular help us to stay connected to the person of Christ as the model for our life.

The other benefit of praying in this fashion is that it gives us a way to be in solidarity and *pray with the church* even though we are alone. It reminds us that no matter how alone we feel, we are never really alone. As we offer prayers that the church has written and prayed for centuries, we are joining with millions of Christians around the world who are praying in the same rhythm in one way or another. Even when we are on retreat, we are part of a much larger reality: the communion of saints made up of those who gone before us, those who are presently alive, and all who will come after us.

This way of praying expresses a deeper unity that transcends all our divisions. As Phyllis Tickle writes,

When one prays the hours, one is using the exact words, phrases, and petitions that informed our faith for centuries. . . . We are using the exact words, phrases, and petitions that were offered just an hour earlier by our fellow Christians in the prior time zone, and that, in an hour will be picked up and offered again in the next time zone. The result is a constant cascade before the throne of God of the "unceasing prayer" to which St. Paul urges us.

How wonderful to contribute to this "constant cascade of unceasing prayer"— at least while on retreat.

Once you have experienced fixed-hour prayer on retreat, you might even be inspired to incorporate at least some of these prayers into your everyday rhythm back at home.

Fixed-hour prayer expresses a deeper unity that transcends all our divisions.

Practicing RETREAT

Preparing for retreat. If you already practice fixed-hour prayer, plan to continue your practice, perhaps with some enhancements since you will have more time. If you have never prayed this way before, retreat is the perfect time to try it! Make it a part of your preparations to ask about what the community provides; then you can plan to enter fully into whatever rhythms are a part of the community's life and add whatever else God might be inviting you to. By participating in the community's prayer schedule, you will experience rhythms of solitude and come together in community even as you maintain your silence. If the community doesn't provide fixed-hour prayer, you can set up your own structure by bringing along a resource to help you establish and engage in this rhythm. (See appendix one for suggested resources to bring with you, or that can help you continue this rhythm of prayer back at home.)

While on retreat. If you already practice fixed-hour prayer, continue that on retreat by doing what you normally do or by participating with the community in what they are doing (preferable). You may want to set your intention ahead of time that you will trust God to bring the right invitations to you through the community and whatever spiritual direction is offered. This kind of submission is a powerful antidote to our willfulness. Enter into rest by determining you will say yes to God's invitations and then trusting yourself to him. If you do not practice fixed-hour prayer and the community doesn't offer it, explore this as a fresh spiritual discipline by using the prayers provided or one of the prayer books suggested in appendix one.

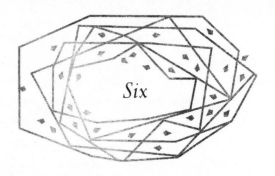

Six

LETTING GO *of* YOUR GRIP

Into your hands I commit my spirit.

JESUS

O N A RECENT PLANE FLIGHT FROM Chicago to Indianapolis, we encountered some of the worst turbulence I have ever experienced. It was so bad that the young woman sitting next to me asked if she could hold my hand—which she gripped tightly for the rest of the flight. She said that it would help if she could talk—which she also did for the rest of the flight. What was ironic is that she had no idea that I am a nervous flyer too, which is putting it mildly! Her fear inspired me to act more bravely than I felt, and somehow we made it through and landed safely. Since then, frequent flyers have told me that such turbulence is fairly normal on this route given the fact that the plane never gets enough altitude to find smooth air on such a short flight; that didn't help much after the fact.

Over the years, I have talked to different people about my fear of flying. It seems most people have ways of thinking about flying that work for them. Intellectual types like to go over the statistics, comparing the number of casualties from flying versus the number of casualties from driving. Apparently the number of deaths from car accidents far exceeds those caused by flying. But that fact makes absolutely no difference in how I feel. Those who understand engineering enjoy talking about aeronautics, how planes are constructed with so many safety features, how safe air travel is today, and so forth. But somehow that doesn't do much to quell such primal fears either. My imagination still runs wild, envisioning all manner of things that could go wrong.

Then there are spiritual director types who like to talk about surrender—that is, trusting oneself to God, imagining God's hand holding the airplane and my life in his hands—literally. Doesn't matter. My palms still sweat at takeoff. My heart races at every little bump. (How can people sleep through that?) I can't concentrate on work or reading while I'm focusing on continuing to breathe. And all I can think about is how bad I am at trusting God—with my life, with my destiny, with my very self.

SWEET SURRENDER

Surrender doesn't come easy to me on any level, and it occurs to me that perhaps people who most need to be in control are the ones who have the most trouble flying, because we are not, well, in control. Perhaps we are the ones who have the most trouble with retreats as well. That's the bad news. The good news is that the spiritual practice of retreat is a primary tool God can use to teach us one of the most basic dynamics of the spiritual life—how to relinquish ourselves to God.

Surrender—or "abandonment to divine providence," as it is called in some of the older writings—is the central dynamic of the spiritual life, and retreat offers us many concrete opportunities for practicing it. The reason this is important is that at some point on retreat most of us will realize, *Oh no! I am not in control anymore!* This is harder for some than for others, but it is a feeling we need to work through in order to fully enter into retreat and experience its full benefit.

To relinquish is to let go ... of human striving and human effort ... of what we usually identify with and how we identify ourselves ... of our addiction to whatever we use to distract ourselves from what needs attention ... of our attempts at controlling everyone and everything. *Relinquishment* is a synonym of *surrender*, and it is what David is talking about in Psalm 46:10 when he says, "Be still [literally, let go of your grip], and know [experiential, full-body knowing] that I am God." Another way to say this might be "Let go of your grip and *experience* letting God be God in your life."

Relinquishment as a defining characteristic of retreat is actually what Emilie Griffin is describing when she says, "Making a retreat requires as certain kind of trust. We need to trust the Spirit. In contrast to vacations or holidays in which activities—planned sight-seeing, sports, entertainment, or events—are within our control, retreat leads us into a less predictable situation. We don't know what God has in store for us, but we are willing to risk what we will find out."

> *Surrender is the central dynamic of the spiritual life, and retreat offers us many concrete opportunities for practicing it.*

So how does this work? What are the inner dynamics of relinquishment, and how does the practice of retreat become a training ground for learning how to surrender ourselves to God?

RELINQUISHING DIRECT INVOLVEMENT

One challenging aspect of "going apart" and being on retreat is that I really am apart—cut off from—those I love most or things I think are really important. The lives of my loved ones go on without my knowledge or direct involvement. The work and ministry I am a part of goes on without me. World events go on without my knowledge, and if I am truly retreating, I even miss the news—which is uncomfortable at times and a blessing at others! Being out of the loop is both hard and good.

Part of what gives me pause here is that I was actually on retreat on 9/11, and those of us who were there together didn't hear about what was happening until hours after the jets had crashed into the World Trade Center!

On one retreat I remember hitting a point when the discomfort of being apart actually became quite acute as I pondered how much life was going on without me. I was missing out on a grandson's fifth birthday party and being present to witness my daughter's creativity, checking in daily with another daughter who was pregnant, accompanying my dear parents to a medical appointment, dealing with a hard situation in our ministry community, going for evening walks with my husband. I simply wasn't there, and in order to be on retreat I had to accept this.

Two things help me with this. One is the conviction that there has to be something in my life that is fairly concrete that enables me to keep God in his rightful place as first love in my life. How many times have I been hesitant (or flat-out refused) to go on retreat—even when I knew I needed it and that God was inviting me to it—because I was inordinately attached to certain aspects of my life and my place in it all? While I realize that a fair portion of my commitment to my family and other responsibilities is good, some of it indicates a disordered attachment. In other words, I have allowed these attachments to supersede my attachment to God and my willingness to say yes to his invitations in my life.

One of the primary ways we show we love and value the people in our lives is by giving them time, a certain quality (and sometimes even a quantity) of time characterized by giving them our full and undivided attention. If you think about it, this is what retreat *is*, where God is concerned; it is one way we cultivate our love for God and keep our relationship with God primary. It is an opportunity to remember and to *live* what we often forget—that we belong to God differently than we belong to our spouse, our girlfriend or boyfriend, our children, our parents, our best friend, our church, or a business or ministry we have founded. Retreat helps us to keep the *ultimate reality* of our lives ultimate.

> *Retreat is one way we cultivate our love for God and keep our relationship with God primary.*

THE MINISTRY OF ABSENCE

The other thing that helps me deal with my compulsion to control things through my direct involvement and my fear of missing out is what Henri Nouwen has called "the ministry of absence." Jesus modeled this for his disciples as he prepared them for the fact that he would be leaving them. He explained to them that once he was no longer with them physically, he would be even closer to them through the Holy Spirit he was asking his Father to send. He made the bold statement that his departure would be *to their advantage* because then the Holy Spirit would come, enabling him to be closer to them at all times and in all ways. They thought Jesus was crazy, and they had a hard time grasping what he was trying to tell them—that "in [his] absence a new and more intimate presence became possible, a presence which nurtured and sustained . . . and created a desire to see him again." Could the same be true for us as well?

In his book *Henri Nouwen and Spiritual Polarities*, Wil Hernandez points out that "what Nouwen is specifically advocating for is an act of 'creative withdrawal.' The rationale for such withdrawal is to pave the way for the Spirit of God to work freely in a person or situation without us potentially getting in the way. In short, we have to leave so that the Spirit can come." I don't know about you, but I have a tendency to think that being physically present and always available is the only way to do anyone any good. This is grandiosity, plain and simple; Jesus shows us another way. He shows us that sometimes we can do more for people in our absence than we can do for them in our presence. Nouwen encourages us to consider the possibility of presence *in* absence, and as I have tried to lean into this truth, I have experienced several things:

1. On retreat I am drawn more deeply into prayer for those I love and the situations I care about than in my more limited times of solitude, silence, and prayer in the rhythm of normal life. And it's not so much prayer with words as it is being present to God on others' behalf. As I am more fully present to the presence of God within, invariably God brings those I love into that space, and we simply sit there together allowing the caring love of God to permeate everything.

2. I am drawn into a more incisive sense of knowing *what to pray for*—what is most needed in the person's life or in the situation I am praying for. I am able to sense the beyond-words groaning of the Holy Spirit for that person and join God in that prayer. This is a richer and more substantive way of being present than fluttering around trying to do things for people all the time. And it's a lot more restful too.

3. I see how (unknowingly) I try to take the place of God in people's lives by being more present and involved than I need to be. I am open to consider that, when I am away on retreat, perhaps my

absence creates space for God to be God in their lives too! Without me there—always guiding, directing, comforting, helping, giving advice, solving problems, manipulating situations, controlling outcomes—perhaps they will turn to God and allow God to meet them rather than relying on me. And that is good! Plus, I get to practice deeper levels of trust in God, not only for myself but for others.

This is not say that we pray *instead of* being present and active in people's lives and in situations that need our loving engagement. Not at all! The depth of prayer that takes place on retreat prepares me to reengage when the time is right, but to do so more wisely, more lovingly, and less compulsively than how I typically engage. And that is what the people around me need most!

Sometimes we can do more for people in our absence than we can do for them in our presence.

Practicing RETREAT

Preparing for retreat. Part of preparing for retreat is to schedule it in a loving way that honors commitments you have made to others while making sure you get a retreat sometimes. If I were to wait until there was a time when I wouldn't miss anything, I would never take a retreat. As you look at your calendar with a view to scheduling your retreat, be prepared to practice relinquishing direct involvement and embrace the ministry of absence. Talk to God about this and let God guide you in this tender place. Be as loving as you can as you prepare others for your absence. Help them understand what you are doing. Let them know how much you love them and that this is not so much about leaving them as it is about being present to God. Tell them you are planning to disconnect from your technology (a radical choice!), but give them an emergency number they can use if they need to reach you.

While on retreat. Use your retreat time to practice relinquishing direct involvement and embracing the ministry of absence. When you feel sad about what you're missing, afraid of missing out, or concerned about loved ones, reread this chapter and journal your response. Open yourself to what God is teaching you about the ministry of absence, and use this as an opportunity to hold those you love in God's presence, trusting his presence in their lives too.

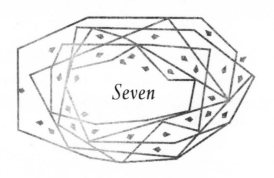

Seven

RELINQUISHING FALSE-SELF PATTERNS

*Every movement toward the humiliation of the
false self, if we accept it, is a step toward
interior freedom and inner resurrection.*

FATHER THOMAS KEATING

— ♦ ◆

W HEN I TOOK MY FIRST EXTENDED RETREAT over twenty
years ago, it was under the able guidance of the folks at the
Shalem Institute—a group of people I respect and hoped to continue
with in my training as a spiritual director. At the time, I was on staff
at a large, high-profile church working in the area of spiritual formation, and I had already become aware that whenever I included this
bit of information as I introduced myself, people seemed to sit up and
take a little bit more notice. They seemed more interested in me, or at
least intrigued and curious. Sometimes they would even ask if we
could get together and talk about how spiritual formation fit in the
church I was a part of, and the attention felt pretty good!

The only problem is that those kinds of conversations and connections were not what I was on retreat for, so I had mixed feelings about this. On the one hand, I kind of liked the extra attention. But on the other hand, I noticed that being recognized in this way compromised my ability to be on retreat—to simply rest and relinquish myself to God. Once people knew who I was, I was no longer anonymous and felt I needed to watch myself a little more carefully to be sure I was presenting myself in ways that were consistent with my role and any expectations that created. A subtle sense of needing to be more *on* and live up to others' expectations crept in. Of course, this worked against the basic purpose of retreat and my deepest longing—to rest from all that and just be a soul in God's presence.

WHO ARE YOU?

When I returned to the Shalem Institute to begin a two-year training program within a cohort, I knew we would be introducing ourselves in the larger group and I would have an important choice to make: by mentioning my ministry setting, I could influence how people viewed me, which would make me feel a little more special. Or I could choose *not* identify myself by this external role in order to maintain needed privacy and to engage the group just as a person apart from any curiosity or expectation that might come from this identifying detail. Choosing to remain anonymous felt like an important invitation for me, and yet I was surprised at how hard it was. To my chagrin, I had to acknowledge that I depended on external roles and titles to define me a whole lot more than I wanted to admit, and in fact I used it to shore up an uncertain and fragile sense of self!

So here was an excellent opportunity for another level of relinquishment. I could choose to let go of defining myself by external factors and enter into this experience simply as the seeker I know myself to be. It was one way I could actually rest from the pressure of being defined by roles, responsibilities, and achievements. The clear invitation was to relinquish myself and my identity to God, rather than succumbing to the urge to manipulate how people viewed me. This turned out to be a challenging discipline, but in the end it created a transformative opportunity—to *practice* rooting my identity in God and God alone.

SHE HAS DONE WHAT SHE COULD

For years I have dreamed of having Jesus' words to Mary recorded in Mark 14 inscribed on my tombstone: "Leave her alone. . . . She has done what she could" (NLT). This is partly tongue in cheek—a slightly cynical perspective on my life that comes out when expectations seem impossible to manage. But make no mistake: my dreams about this epitaph speak volumes about how I experience my life and my makeup. Driven by a quirky cocktail of God-given passion, internal compulsions, and external expectations, the idea that I might someday reach a point where Jesus actually says to others in my hearing, "Leave her alone, she has done what she could" seems like a moment worth aspiring to!

I shared this with a spiritual director once, asking tearfully, "How will I know when I've done enough? I just want to know when I've done enough." Clearly he did not take me as seriously as I was taking myself because he said with a godly smirk, "What if your tombstone says, 'She did *more* than she could'?" I pondered that for a good long time—especially the implication that I was bringing some of this on myself!

Many of us have no idea how addicted we are to human striving, hard work, and performance-oriented drivenness until we actually stop. This may be one of the most shocking realities we face while on retreat: There is a direct correlation between *the discomfort* we feel when we cease our relentless human striving and our *addiction* to activity and achievement as a way of staving off feelings of inner emptiness. In fact, we could almost predict that those who are most uncomfortable with the nonactivity of retreat are probably most addicted to activity as a way of avoiding inner emptiness and shoring up their sense of self with external accomplishments.

To say no to our compulsive doing is uncomfortable in the short term, but relinquishment is the invitation. True inner retreat requires that we relinquish all our attempts to fill the void in the usual ways so we can peer into the abyss of our loneliness and emptiness long enough to find God there.

> *True inner retreat requires that we relinquish all our attempts to fill the void in the usual ways so we can peer into the abyss of our loneliness and emptiness long enough to find God there.*

BEYOND PRODUCTIVITY

Another one of the great ironies of retreat is that overachievers tend to approach retreat as a place to get something done. I cannot tell you how many times I have gone on retreat seriously intending to be on retreat but also secretly hoping that I would accomplish something—everything from writing thank you notes to getting books checked off my reading list, to finishing a major book project! I'm hoping I can get two for the price of one—get a retreat *and* get something done. But it just doesn't work that way; when we fool ourselves into attempting to be productive on retreat, we leave more exhausted than when we came.

Even if we are able to set aside our obsession with productivity in the outer world, we might be tempted to watch ourselves while on retreat to see if anything is happening and to evaluate whether we are "making progress" spiritually. If this happens, we need to shut it down right away. Dallas Willard offers this wisdom:

Even lay down your ideas as to what solitude and silence are supposed to accomplish in your spiritual growth. You will discover incredibly good things. One is that you have a soul. Another, that God is near and the universe is brimming with goodness. Another, that others aren't as bad as you often think. But don't try to discover these or you won't. You'll just be busy and find more of your own business.

The cure for too-much-to-do is solitude and silence, for there you find you are safely more than what you do.... You will know this finding of your soul and God is happening by an increased sense of who you are and a lessening of the feeling that you *have* to do this, that, or the other thing. That harassing, hovering feeling of "have to" largely comes from the vacuum in your soul, where you ought to be at home with your Father in his kingdom. As the vacuum is rightly filled, you will increasingly know that you do not have to do those things—not even those things you want to do.

Wow. Read that quote twice if you need to. By relinquishing normal patterns of human striving and hard work, we can become aware of the vacuum we keep trying to fill by doing stuff and achieving things. With enough inner stamina (from having rested) and enough outer support (from the retreat environment) we may be able to refuse our tendency to reflexively fill the vacuum in all the normal ways and instead allow the fullness of God to seep in, which is satisfying beyond anything we could have done for ourselves.

PRACTICING RELINQUISHMENT ON RETREAT

Many of us are deeply, hauntingly aware of our false-self patterns, all the ways we have learned how to avoid relinquishing ourselves to God. This awareness might have been aided by working with a variety of tools designed to help us with this: a twelve-step program, the

Myers-Briggs, the Enneagram, the seven deadly sins, a 360 performance review at work, or psychological insights gained through therapy. Whatever has contributed to your self-awareness, consider the false-self patterns you are most aware of *right now* and ponder what it might look like to practice relinquishing those patterns while on retreat.

Using the Enneagram and Richard Rohr's descriptions of the nine patterns by which human beings attempt to secure their survival and avoid their primal anxieties, consider how you might relinquish your normal patterns on retreat. Interestingly enough, the following patterns correspond quite closely with the seven deadly sins if you would rather look at it that way. However you choose to get in touch with these primal instincts and observe their hold on your life, ask, *What would it look like for me to relinquish myself to God on retreat as it relates to my false-self patterns?*

Type One. The need to be good and perfect. On retreat, consider giving up any attempt to "get it right." Rather than asking how things might be improved, just enter trusting that this is what God has for you. If there is anything about your retreat time or the retreat house or the retreat schedule or the retreat leadership that you feel is lacking or could be done better, relinquish your impulse to fix it or to improve on anything and receive it as it is. Let it be good enough in God's hands. And let yourself be good enough too. Resist the urge to have a perfect retreat or to turn this into a self-improvement project. Experiencing the pure beauty and wildness of nature also can be deeply moving for *ones* because they don't have to fix anything. Everything is perfect just as it is, which gives them a connection with "holy rightness," meeting their divine longing for the perfection and completeness of God.

Type Two. The need to be needed. Notice how it feels to be served rather than to serve. How comfortable or uncomfortable is this for you? Rather than focusing so much on what you can do for others, be present to your own needs, trusting God to meet you in that place. Receive the care and service others provide as God caring for your needs. When the impulse to help or to serve others comes upon you, can you relinquish that impulse and instead ask God to show you what you might be avoiding *within yourself* that needs attention, love, and care?

Type Three. The need to succeed. Determine not to manage your image at all while on retreat, including any subtle ways of advertising yourself by talking about your roles, titles, accomplishments, or the book you're writing. Notice how comfortable or uncomfortable this feels. Sit in your cell and notice your sense of self (or the lack of it) beyond all your doing—even if it's uncomfortable. Be vigilant about your tendency to appear more put together than you are and to turn even this retreat time into a project, a place of productivity, *or a success story*. Relinquish such impulses to God. Lay them down and just be.

Type Four. The need to be special. As you arrive and move through this retreat time, notice any attempts to draw attention to yourself—flashy clothes, dramatic makeup and jewelry, how you introduce yourself to others, whether you expect or demand special treatment. Relinquish these attempts to be seen as special and sit with whatever you feel. (I remember asking a female *four* on retreat to come to a spiritual direction session without her makeup on—just once—so she could experience being a bit more real and less dramatic. It became a turning point!) Face the undercurrent of sadness and emptiness that often runs beneath everything. Mourn your losses. Follow the schedule and guidelines set for the retreat rather than giving in to the feeling that you are so special you don't need to! Be normal and experience how special that is.

Type Five. The need to perceive. Since *fives* rely on information and knowledge in order to feel safe, preferring to hold themselves back and observe, choose to engage fully. Relinquish your need for more information and enter into whatever experiences are offered on retreat—whether you understand them or not. Feel your feelings. Cry your tears. Get a massage or do something else that helps you be in your body. Relinquish your emotional stinginess and give yourself fully to God. Believe that *experiencing* God may be more important than knowing more about God. And let go of your reading list!

Type Six. The need for security. By nature, *sixes* prefer structures and beliefs that help them feel secure; they are typically afraid to risk moving outside the external sources that provide them with this feeling of security, which can make the risky invitation of retreat feel rather challenging. Since your posture toward new people and ideas is often mistrust, you will tend to engage retreat with questions such as, Is the theology of the person who is teaching right? Am I using the right prayers? Am I saying them right? Is it okay to take communion differently from how I've been taught? Is the Enneagram Christian or is it a tool of the devil? See if you can let this go. Notice what you're afraid of and choose it anyway. If a teaching challenges your theology, open up and wonder whether God might have something for you. When you feel anxious, identify the fear underneath and choose to trust God *right there in that place*. Let the unpredictability of retreat time be your invitation to trust God and trust your own inner authority.

Type Seven. The need to avoid pain. *Sevens* typically avoid retreat because they prefer to be surrounded by fun and laughter, pleasure and positive thinking. They tend to skate along the surface of things, ignoring the more painful aspects of life. The invitation for *sevens* on retreat is to relinquish superficial addiction to pleasure in favor of the deeper joy that comes through communion with God in all of life— even the painful aspects. Since you are prone to addictive behavior, choose to leave your addictions behind in order to face reality head-on rather than avoiding it. Pack simply and limit your options. Feel your pain. Cry your tears. Experience the simple joy of silence, sunsets, a hot shower, sitting in the warm sun, a morning walk, having a meal prepared for you—without all the external props and stimulation. Face your dark side and find God there.

Type Eight. The need to be against. Since *eights* love being against and may even go so far as to create conflict because they feel more comfortable in a fight, your invitation is to relinquish that fighting spirit and simply submit yourself to the good that is at hand. Notice your tendency to want to take the opposite side of everything and just go with what's going for once! Trust that good things can happen in the peace and quiet, not just when you're fighting something. Also (and this will be hard) experience your weakness, your tenderness, and your vulnerability. Be a child in God's presence. When the tears come, don't be afraid that you are going soft; instead receive tears as the gift they are, an indication that you are soft in the best way: soft and malleable toward God and what he is doing in you.

Type Nine. The need to avoid. It is possible that retreat might be easiest for *nines* because they seek to avoid everything: life, the world, evil and good, and maybe even themselves. They hate conflict and may give in to desire for peace at any price—even within themselves. For *nines*, retreat can be an opportunity to renounce laziness and get in touch with God-given passion and purpose—that which will get them off the couch, in touch with their giftedness, and willing to contribute their gifts in the world. Retreat is a time when they may be invited to relinquish their deep desire to avoid conflict and notice those places where God might be asking them to come forward and fight for something that matters. As Rohr says, "It helps nines when they consciously struggle to find their own standpoint instead of always orienting themselves toward others."

That's a lot of relinquishment, and at this point you may be wondering why we would lay down so much that feels essential to our survival. The answer is simple. We relinquish all these things so we can release ourselves more fully to God. As frightening as relinquishment sounds, the result is spiritual freedom—the freedom to be what and who God is calling me to be—not who I have been unconsciously programmed to be, who others are telling me to be, or even who I am determined to be. This is our true self in God, totally abandoned to the One who loves us—on retreat and always.

As frightening as relinquishment sounds, the result is spiritual freedom.

Practicing RETREAT

Preparing for retreat or while on retreat. If you know your Enneagram number, take a look at the description of what relinquishment might look for you or go deep into your own soul and ask how God might be guiding you to take next steps in relinquishing yourself to the divinity while on retreat.

Jot it down. If you do not know what your type is, don't worry about it. My guess is that something in the previous descriptions resonated with you and that letting go in that way and surrendering yourself to God points the way to a freedom you have been seeking. Jot down whatever words or phrases describe a place of unfreedom in you. Then, be as concrete as you can about how you might follow that path toward greater freedom.

If, while on retreat, you sense the impulse to control your experience in some way that feels old and familiar, but not in a good way, experience this as God's invitation to abandon yourself to divine providence and just do it!

Prayer of Abandonment

Father,
I abandon myself
Into your hands;
Do with me what you will.
For whatever you may do, I thank you.

I am ready for all,
I accept all.

Let only your will be done in me
as in all your creatures.
I wish no more than this, O Lord.

Into your hands
I commend my soul.
I offer it to you
With all the love of my heart.
For I love you, my God,
and I so need to give myself,
to surrender myself
into your hands,
without reserve,
and with boundless confidence,
for you are my Father.

Charles de Foucauld, 1858–1916

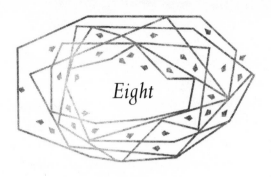

Eight

SPACE *for* DISCERNMENT

*To know God's will is to actively claim an
intimate relationship with God.*

HENRI NOUWEN

❧ ❧ ❧

O N RETREAT I USUALLY START every day (before breakfast even) with a spacious time of silence in which I am open and receptive to whatever God might bring. (There is always coffee involved!) My daily practice of spending shorter times in solitude has prepared me for this. While it might feel like I'm doing nothing, I am doing what is most important: letting the chaos settle. Waiting on God. Resting in God. Allowing God to be God in my life. For a hard-driving leader and controller of outcomes, this is no small thing! In fact, it is transforming.

As we are quiet, questions and areas for discernment will naturally come to heart and mind, and God might even surface some we hadn't thought of. Silence offers us a way to receive them but stop short of striving too hard to answer them. Even though we may have brought prepared questions with us, sometimes truer questions need to be allowed to surface. It takes courage to allow God to address us with questions and then to let God lead in how and when they get dealt with. Silence is the symbol and the reality of letting God take the initiative with us and receiving what God brings rather than orchestrating everything for ourselves. In silence we can actually discern the movements of God's spirit rather than doing everything ourselves.

> *In silence we can actually discern the movements of God's spirit rather than doing everything ourselves.*

SILENCE AND RECEPTIVITY

Many of us are in danger of moving through life so fast there is little or no time for this kind of attention; because we are so riled up, we find it increasingly difficult if not impossible to settle into a quiet, listening stance in which God can speak to us about matters of great importance. We are chagrined to admit we are moving so fast we routinely find ourselves making decisions totally apart from the awareness of God in our lives or any clear sense of divine leading. This means we are relying on our own wisdom rather discerning what is on God's heart for us more often than we think. This is an alarming situation for any Christian—given the fact that human wisdom is often so different than God's wisdom on any number of things (see 1 Corinthians 1:25; 2:1-5).

Discernment is *an increasing capacity to recognize and respond to the presence and activity of God—both in the ordinary moments of our lives and in the decisions we face.* The word *increasing* indicates that we will never fully arrive when it comes to discernment, but we *can* grow more and more attuned to the presence and will of God through practice. *Recognizing* and *responding* are related but separate ideas.

To *recognize* is to see, to know, to cherish, and to allow the other to speak; then to *respond* truly and thoughtfully requires that we bring our best and most attentive selves. Of course, we will need to *recognize* the presence and activity of God before we can *respond*, but for a whole host of reasons it is possible to recognize what God is doing and yet refuse to participate. So the idea is to recognize *and* respond, and if we don't, we could be curious about why we are not responding and what's holding us back. It is one thing to be aware that God is present with us all the time; it is quite another to recognize God's activity in our lives and seek to join God in whatever God is up to.

Learning to find God in the ordinary fosters within us *the habit* of discernment, resulting in hard-won wisdom we can then bring to bear on *the practice* of discernment when we are facing life-shaping decisions. When we face choices we believe will affect the outcome of our lives, our desire is to make that decision in God, opening ourselves to God's wisdom. During such times we need extended retreat time in order to pay attention to the questions and inner dynamics that will help us discern God's wisdom and direction. We need something more than human wisdom in order to choose well, *and* we need quiet in order to listen for this wisdom.

Learning to find God in the ordinary fosters within us the habit of discernment.

LETTING THE CHAOS SETTLE

One of the first things we may notice on retreat is how hard it is to get quiet on the inside, to allow the inner chaos to settle so we can actually hear something! Even though we have worked hard to arrive and we desire to say yes to God's invitations and receive what God has for us, it's not always as easy as it sounds! When external noise has been silenced, we might become aware that the chaos isn't just *out there* in the world we've left behind—it's also *in here* because of all we bring with us. Most of us have been running so hard and so fast for so long that entering into retreat feels like coming to a screeching halt after driving much too fast; our rpms are still at racing levels and there might even be skid marks and the smell of burning tires!

So here's my suggestion: even though you may be aware of the deep questions and desperate desires you have brought with you, resist the urge to think too hard, work too hard, or in any other way try to force God's hand. Instead, enter more deeply into a posture of trust, believing that what is most needed will be given in God's way and in God's time. Begin your retreat day (or each day) by being with God in silent receptivity for a time. You don't have to sit; you can choose to take a slow, sensing walk in which you aren't trying to get anywhere, but instead to go where God takes you. Start letting go of your attempts to make something happen, loosening your grip on your own agenda and allowing the inner chaos to settle so eventually you *can* hear and receive at God's initiative. Sitting or walking in silent openness is a way to begin practicing trust that God will do what is needed in God's time.

DISCERNING GOD'S PRESENCE IN THE ORDINARY

As I entered into an extended retreat recently, I knew I was desperate for rest, but I was also aware of several areas in which I desperately wanted and needed to pay attention to God. The first was a desire to find God's presence and wisdom in my ordinary life, which had changed so much and so quickly that I had not had the time to make full sense of it all or to discern God's call in it. My husband and I are blessed with three daughters, who are all married and have their own children. All live nearby, along with my sweet parents, who are navigating the aging process. Over the last ten years nine grandchildren have been born in quick succession—blessed events, all—making our family life full. Opportunities to be involved meaningfully with children, grandchildren, and parents are endless. At the same time, the demands and opportunities of my vocational life have grown. This is my ordinary life, and I have been increasingly aware of a deep longing to discern God's presence in it and to be in touch with a deeper wisdom for how to navigate life.

On some days I feel I'm doing pretty well at being present to my life and its many blessings, but on other days the choices about how to live well and give energy and attention to all these gifts and priorities can be agonizing. No amount of human wisdom fully addresses my longings, concerns, and need for wisdom regarding how to navigate my ordinary life. It is a place where only God's wisdom will do.

As I carried my longing for God's wisdom and guidance into retreat and simply held it in God's presence, a prayer emerged: "God, help me see my life as you see it and myself in it as you see me." That prayer stayed with me and prayed itself in me the whole time; it was immensely helpful. When I wanted to figure things out through my own human striving, this prayer helped me "cease striving" and allow God to bring what was needed—in his own way in his own time. As I held this question throughout retreat time, I was grateful God gave me a way to pray that helped me *be with it* in God's presence, to even rest with it in God's presence rather than trying so hard to solve it. Gradually and without even knowing exactly how or when it happened, God gave me a way of seeing my life that bought more peace and confidence.

SOMETHING NOT QUITE RIGHT

Another desire drew me into retreat as well, and it had to do with what Scripture calls "testing the spirits." For quite some time I had had a sense that something was not quite right in one aspect of my ministry life, and I couldn't tell if it was something not quite right outside myself or if somehow I was projecting my own darkness onto someone else. This is complicated stuff, and I needed time, space, and good spiritual direction to "test the spirits to see whether they are from God" (1 John 4:1). Through years of teaching and interaction with the Enneagram, I was also aware of needing and wanting more specific insights into my own false-self patterns—how they are constantly at work in my life and how they were affecting the people I care about and my ministry. I wanted to discern if there was something inside me that needed to surrender *or* if the desolation I was experiencing signaled some sort of danger to be avoided.

Learning to pay attention and test the spirits within and without is another way to talk about discernment; it is a mark of Christian maturity, which means we can all cultivate it. One of the ways we cultivate this capacity is by recognizing the subtle inner dynamics beneath the surface chop of our emotions and relationships; this requires becoming quiet enough to get in touch with the reality underneath. On retreat we cultivate our God-given ability to discern the difference between good and evil so we can choose the good.

It might seem rather jarring to use the words *good* and *evil*, because in our current cultural milieu we don't know what they mean. The word *good* has come to mean nothing because it has been so overused, and the word *evil* seems so harsh and judgmental that no one feels comfortable using it. We need to reclaim these words, however, because they are biblical words that matter as we seek to become more discerning. In the context of discernment, *good* means that which is from God, leads us toward God, and leads to greater freedom for our authentic self in God. The word *evil* means that which is not from God, that which leads us away from God and our most authentic self in God.

Retreat is an ideal time to drop beneath the surface and pay attention to the *spirit* of things in my life—where I am moving toward the good and where I might need to move away from evil. Retreat is a wonderful opportunity to do a scan of your ordinary life in order to increase your awareness of God's presence and how God is leading you. The following questions can help us with discerning God's presence in the ordinary:

Retreat is an ideal time to drop beneath the surface and pay attention to the spirit of things in my life—where I am moving toward the good and where I might need to move away from evil.

- Where does God seem most present in my life these days? When and where have I had the strongest sense of God with me and for me?

- What in my present life situation is leading me toward God and others in love? What is leading me away?

- What is the underlying spirit in my dealings with others and their dealings with me? Is there any spirit that feels uncomfortable and warrants further attention?

- What is going on in my life these days, spiritually speaking? Where does there seem to be the greatest surrender to love, peace that passes understanding (even in the midst of difficulty), freedom for my authentic self, and life-giving energy and vitality? What seem to be obstacles to surrender, peace that passes understanding, and so on?

- What guidance emerges from this awareness—particularly as I seek to align myself more fully with God's purposes? When and where have I sensed God's clear leading?

If you are reading this on retreat, stop here and spend time reflecting on God's presence in your ordinary life before going on.

DISCERNING GOD'S GUIDANCE IN DECISION MAKING

We always have decisions to make, whether we perceive them to be major life-changing ones or those that will give shape to our lives gradually, over time. Even though Jesus lived in perfect unity with his Father, he retreated often to a quiet place to listen to the voice of God regarding decisions and directions he was taking. Of all people who might have been able to convince themselves they did not need to retreat in order to hear God, Jesus would have fit the bill. But instead we see him regularly retreating to the mountain, into the wilderness, across the lake, and into the garden in order to stay in tune with God's heart and plan for him.

In times of discernment, the questions we are willing to ask ourselves (or allow God to ask of us) are often more important than the answers we think we know. If we are bringing an issue for discernment, retreat time creates space for pondering different kinds of questions than we are able to address while we are on the fly. Do not approach the following points as a list to complete; rather, scan this list and then go to the question (or two or three) you are drawn to and spend your time with those.

Direction and calling. How does this choice fit with the overall direction and calling of God upon my life? (You may want to reflect on Jeremiah's experience of suppressing his calling in Jeremiah 20:9.) What word or phrase captures my sense of calling these days, and would this choice enable me to continue living into my calling? Note: Sometimes we are inordinately attached to a certain way of expressing our calling or a certain context in which we want to express it. We can be quite willful in clinging to the specifics. It can be clarifying to separate the context or *the specific way* we might express our calling from the calling itself.

Consolation and desolation. Which choice brings the deepest sense of life, inner peace, and freedom for love (Deuteronomy 30:11-14; John 10:10; Philippians 4:7; 2 Corinthians 3:17)? Is there a growing sense of wholeness, authenticity, congruence with who I am in God? Does this choice (or some aspect of it) confuse me, drain life from me, or leave me feeling disconnected from God, from love, from my most authentic self?

Desire. Spend time reflecting on the story of the healing of blind Bartimaeus in Mark 10:46-52. If Jesus were standing before me and asked, "What do you want me to do for you?" how would I respond?

Scripture. Is there a particular Scripture God is bringing to me relative to this choice—especially one that is surprising and unplanned: a reading from the lectionary, a Scripture reading in a church service, something offered by a friend? Use retreat time to sit with that Scripture and ponder, *What is it saying to me in the midst of this decision?*

Life of Christ. Is this choice consistent with what I know about the mind and heart of Christ and his redemptive purposes in the world? Is there any aspect of Jesus' life God is bringing to mind, and how does it speak to the question I am discerning?

Character growth and spiritual formation. Where is God most clearly at work in my character and spiritual transformation? Which choice would give God the most opportunity to nurture this growth and keep me on that growing edge?

Love. How will this direction nurture the fruit of the Spirit in me— particularly the fruit of love? What does love call for? What would be the most loving choice for myself and for those around me?

Clarify my perspective. Take a step forward and then take a step back. *Step forward*—Does this choice value what is eternal and per- manent, and does it hold the deepest value rather than what is tran- sient and impermanent? If I imagine myself on my death bed, which choice would I wish I had made? *Step back*—Jeremiah 6:16 encourages us to actually stop and

> stand at the crossroads, and look,
>   and ask for the ancient paths,
> where the good way lies; and walk in it,
>   and find rest for your souls.

Is there "a good way" that actually feels more restful because it is con- sistent with the whole of your life?

Community. How does this choice fit with others' observations of who I am and what God is doing in my life? Am I willing to open every facet of this decision to a trusted spiritual friend or spiritual director for their wisdom and insight? If not, why? (Unwillingness to open an area of discernment to our trusted community is a red flag.)

Communion of the saints. Is there anything in my own tradition or in the overall tradition of the Christian faith that might inform my decision?

Be alert to "the second spiritual situation." St. Ignatius wisely points out that holiness of life, even great holiness of life, does not eliminate the need for discernment of spirits; rather, it is precisely goodness of life that calls for the "greater discernment of spirits" found in Ignatius's second set of rules.

> A point may come on the spiritual journey when persons who deeply love God must be aware of, understand, and reject certain attractions to good and holy things that, if undertaken, would distract them from the different good and holy things to which God is genuinely calling them. . . .
>
> They will need to discern between spiritual consolation that is authentically of the good spirit and deceptive spiritual consolation that is not of the good spirit, and that will lead, if followed, to spiritual harm.

Simply knowing that such a situation exists is already a great gift; in the stillness of retreat time and, hopefully, with good spiritual direction, we are able to distinguish between what is truly good and what is temptation from the evil one, who may be using good opportunities to distract us from what God is really calling us to.

DISCERNING GOD'S PRESENCE ON RETREAT

Finally, discernment calls us to be attentive to how God is present and is guiding us within our retreat time. Let me share an example. When

I go on retreat I take lots of books. I have a long-time love of reading and there are so many things I am interested in learning about. Having time to read things I am drawn to but have not had a chance to engage is such a delicious opportunity. Of course, I am disciplined about what I take with me on retreat—only things that are for my own soul, not for my work. But given the nature of my work, there is a fine line between the two! Technically, a spiritual retreat should only include a Bible, a journal, and maybe one book God is using in our lives, but honesty compels me to admit that I usually take several. So as I prepared to go on a recent retreat, I did what I usually do and packed several books for spiritual reading I thought God might want to use during this time. I also told God that I was committed to following every divine invitation that came my way.

At this particular retreat center, we were asked to make our own beds with the linens provided. When I moved the bed out from the wall in order to make it, there was a book from the retreat center library on the prayer of *examen*. (I kid you not!) The author

> *Discernment calls us to be attentive to how God is present and is guiding us within our retreat time.*

was one I knew and valued, but I had never read this particular work. I went with it. Also, my spiritual director on this retreat was a Jesuit priest who was well read and a teacher at heart. He kept pulling books off his shelf that were penetrating and pertinent to the topics I was bringing for discernment. I took this also as a part of God's guidance while on retreat and ended up reading several books cover to cover (with great benefit) without reading anything I'd brought.

I felt like God was my spiritual director leading me to unexpected gifts and resolutions while leaving other things unexplored and unresolved. Retreat teaches us to trust God with that. And that's where things get exciting!

DISCERNMENT AS RELATIONSHIP

I know a married couple who plan a getaway weekend once a year for the specific purpose of talking about their finances and making decisions regarding the upcoming year. When I first heard this, I was aghast! *Why waste a weekend away on such a distasteful subject?* I wondered. My tendency would be to declare such a topic off-limits during a romantic getaway—but that's just me. My friends, however, have discovered a better way.

Over the years they have noticed that the topic of finances is difficult for them, fraught with potential pitfalls due to differences in their personalities, their upbringing, and so on. Through disappointing interactions on this topic in the past, they have learned that getting away from the stress of normal life with its relentless distractions and having a more spacious and relaxed schedule in a setting conducive to listening—to each other and to God—sets them up to be their best selves as they discuss such an important matter. They have discovered that in the right setting, a topic that might be difficult or volatile, or that requires sustained listening and focus can actually become a source of intimacy; their bond is strengthened as they discern together.

The same is true of our relationship with God. There are times when we simply must remove ourselves from our normal existence in order to deal with important matters together. If we don't carve out time and space for this, we risk making decisions out of the worst version of ourselves. Even if the topic at hand is challenging or uncomfortable, what is most needed is to be present to the topic and to God, with our best, most rested selves, and *listen carefully* in the context of such a loving relationship. You'd be surprised what your soul wants to say to God, and you'd be surprised at what God wants to say to your soul.

Practicing RETREAT

Preparing for retreat. One of the most important things about retreat as a regular spiritual practice is that, as you notice things in life that you want to pay attention to with God or decisions you are facing that require more quiet reflection, you can bookmark them knowing you will be able to give full attention to them while on retreat. As you become aware of these things, note them and set your intention to bring those into your retreat time. You may want to jot down a few things here.

While on retreat. Notice how you feel drawn (or how God draws you) to each of the following aspects of discernment, and take time to reflect, respond, and even journal about them:

~ *Discern God's presence and activity in your ordinary life.* Is there any burning bush you have wanted to pay special attention to—especially experiences of consolation and desolation, desire and calling, gratitude and grief? Be sure and create space for this using the questions on page 89.

~ *Seeking God's wisdom and discernment regarding a particular decision you might be facing.* Is there a question or a decision you are facing that you want to bring into this retreat time? Which of the questions on pages 90-92 resonate with you as being important? Journal your response to the questions you feel drawn to.

~ *Discerning God's presence within this particular retreat time and following where he leads*—with special openness to the unexpected. Speak to God about your desire to recognize and respond to his presence and activity *while on retreat.* Then be alert and awake to God's invitations—especially the surprising ones—and follow where they lead.

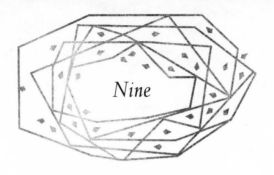

Nine

INVITATION *to* RECALIBRATE

We long to see our lives whole and to know that they matter. We wonder whether our many activities might ever come together in a way of life that is good for ourselves and others. Are we really living in right relation to other people, to the created world, and to God?

CRAIG DYKSTRA AND DOROTHY BASS

◆　◆　◆

SOMETIMES I GET SAD ON RETREAT, which at first surprised me. I think I expected to be happy and at peace the whole time, but this has never been the case. Over time I have gotten used to this, assuming when it comes that my sadness has something to tell me. As I've stayed with the sadness, I've noticed something fairly consistent. On retreat, when I am free from so much distraction, I seem to be more in touch with the deeper desires of my heart; and the sadness often has to do with acknowledging (painfully) that the way I am living is not consistent with those desires.

In the stillness of retreat, I am able to see more clearly how I am being pushed and pulled by other people's expectations, by my own inner compulsions, and by the basic necessities of life in our culture, and I realize how far I've drifted from living my heart's truest desire. It hurts to see this. It exposes the magical thinking that someday I might stumble accidently into a way of life that works but will not require radical choices or disappointing anyone, including myself. Often, by the time I make it to retreat, I feel so overwhelmed and defeated that I convince myself I am at the mercy of forces beyond my control. All of this is uncomfortable. I wonder if perhaps that's at least one of the feelings we're trying to avoid by not going on retreat—the sadness that comes when we realize we are not ordering our lives around what matters most.

On retreat we stop avoiding the pain of the disconnect between our deepest desires and the way we are actually living. We have time and space to reflect on our life rhythms to see if they are really working.

Henri Nouwen reflects on this in his book *Reaching Out.* In his early quest for an authentic spirituality, he observed in himself a frenetic chasing after answers from external sources, resulting in an unsustainable pace of life. He finally concludes, "Maybe my own deep-rooted fear of being on my own

and alone kept me going from person to person, book to book, and school to school, anxiously avoiding the pain of accepting responsibility for my own life." On retreat we stop avoiding the pain of the disconnect between our deepest desires and the way we are actually living. We have time and space to reflect on our life rhythms to see if they are really working.

REFLECTING ON SACRED RHYTHMS

Sacred rhythms are patterns of attitudes, practices, and behaviors set apart for the sacred purpose of keeping us open and available to the transforming presence of Christ. Rather than being a legalistic straight-jacket, these practices and patterns are means of grace that give God access to our souls. The idea of sacred rhythms is rooted in the Christian practice of establishing a *rule of life*—a practice that responds to two questions: *Who do I want to be?* and *How do I want to live?* It might be more accurate to say that a rule of life addresses the interplay between these two questions: *How do I want to live so I can be who I want to be?* Putting an even finer point on it, we might ask, *How do I want to live so I can be the person God created me to be and knows me to be—which is, in the end, who I want to be?*

Hopefully you have worked through a process for establishing your own sacred rhythms and are seeking to live faithfully within them. (For a complete guide in establishing a rule of life, see *Sacred Rhythms*.) Such a process involves getting in touch with your deepest spiritual desires, exploring spiritual practices (such as solitude, silence, prayer, *lectio divina*, self-examination and confession, honoring your body, Sabbath keeping, discernment) that correspond to those desires, and then asking God to guide you in putting them together in a rhythm that works for you. Then, we can make it a regular part of retreat time to step back, reflect on our life patterns, and notice how they are contributing (or not) to our spiritual well-being and the unfolding of God's purposes in our lives. Out of a place of rest *in* God, and as a result of having listened more deeply *to* God, we have the strength and stamina—and even the grace—to reflect honestly on our rule of life/sacred rhythms. We can notice what's working and what's not, what still fits and what might not fit anymore, and most importantly whether or not our sacred rhythms are consistent with desire *as we are experiencing it right now.*

We can notice also what God seems to be up to in our lives and adjust or readjust our way of life for the precise season and function God is calling us to now. Sometimes this involves minor tweaks; other times it's a major overhaul. Things change and life happens. What used to work might not work now. What you wanted then might not be what you want now. And hopefully your desire has deepened and is more clear and focused; over time God may grant increasing measures of courage and resolve to arrange your life for what you say you truly want. As Ron Rolheiser observes, "When we fail to distinguish among the different seasons of our life and how these interface with the challenges and invitations that God and life send us, we are in danger of hurting ourselves in two ways: first, by trying to take on too much when we are not ready for it, and second, by not taking on enough when we are ready for it."

DESIRES GOD LONGS TO MEET

One example of such recalibration and the role desire can play in making significant life changes is the resignation of Pope Benedict XVI. As the first pontiff to step down in six centuries, Benedict said, "'God told me to,' when asked about his decision to dedicate himself to a life of prayer." The eighty-six-year-old pope said he had "undergone a 'mystical experience' during which God gave him the 'absolute desire' to forge a deeper relationship with him." He also said that "the more he witnessed the 'charisma' of his successor, Pope Francis, the more he understood how his stepping aside was the 'will of God.'"

What is interesting to note here is the interplay between what he was aware of deep in his own soul *and* his ability to see the correspondence between that and what God was doing in the world outside of himself. As he became clearer about his own desire *and* this desire was confirmed by what was going on outside of himself, it became evident that it was time for him to recalibrate, to readjust, for God's precise purposes for him at this time. It's not like he had been doing anything wrong before, but that God was initiating a new season, signaled (in part) by awareness of a deeper desire. And that awareness of deeper desire, which he believed was God-given, resulted in significant recalibration. He stepped down as pope to make way for a new pope; this, in turn, made it possible for him to enter into a more secluded life of prayer, silence, and listening—which is what his heart was longing for.

PRIMING THE PUMP

Of course, not all of us will be called to change our lives that radically, and we are not all eighty-six-year-olds called by God into seclusion at the end of a full life in ministry. But we are called to take responsibility for the stewarding of our own lives in response to the desire God has placed within us (Psalm 37:4). The following questions can prime the pump as we seek to reflect on how we are living in relation to desire and whether or not any recalibration is needed:

- What is your rhythm of living with God and with others right now? What's working and what isn't? Are you aware of anything that feels empty or missing? Journal about this.

- What rhythm of living with God and others do you find yourself longing for as you reflect on your life these days? Be honest about this.

- What aspects of your life and practice are most life-giving for you right now? Is there any way God might be inviting you to live into those more fully? Give yourself permission to envision this.

- How would you describe your season of life currently? Has anything significant changed since you last reflected on your rule of life? How have you adjusted for this—or not? Ask God to give you real insight about this.

- What limitations are you challenged by in this season of your life? How have you responded to those? Try to be open and nonjudgmental—even compassionate—with yourself about this rather than harsh and judgmental.

- What unique opportunities for growth and transformation are contained within this season for you? How are you leaning into those or how might you lean into those? Let yourself dream a little here.

- What invitations from God are you most in touch with these days? How can you order your life more intentionally to say yes to those? Do a little brainstorming and planning about this.

- In what ways is God calling you to reclaim, recommit, or recalibrate your rhythms for God's purposes and for the abundance of your own life in this season? Be courageous and claim what God has been saying to you. Trust that the One who is calling you into a more life-giving way of life will be faithful to bring it about.

I keep revisiting a question from Thomas Merton, and I know I will keep returning to it to the end of my days. It is a great one to ponder on retreat: "Ask me not where I live or where I like to eat . . . ask me what I am living for and what is keeping me from living fully for that." This brings us to the topic of our next chapter—finding the freedom to order our lives for what we say we really want.

What is your rhythm of living with God and with others?

Practicing RETREAT

Preparing for retreat. If you have written your rule of life and sense that maybe it is time to recalibrate, be sure to bring it with you.

While on retreat. Take time to notice your life rhythms and how they are working these days. The following questions are not meant to foster feelings of judgment or shame, failure or inadequacy; they are simply to help you reflect clearly on your own sacred rhythms, allowing God to guide you.

1. What are your sacred rhythms these days, and how is God meeting you within them? To what extent do you feel you are arranging your life around what you say you want? What longings stir as you pay attention to this?

2. Describe your practice of solitude and silence as you are experiencing it right now. How do you want to be with God, and how do you sense God wanting to be with you? Is it enough?

3. How are you continuing to cultivate intimacy with God through prayer and listening to God in Scripture? What is the most significant thing God has said to you recently, and how did you respond?

4. What's happening in your body these days? Does anything need attention? If so, what? Are you living in sane rhythms of work and rest? What about Sabbath keeping?

5. What decisions are you facing right now where discernment is truly needed? Are you able to create enough space to get down to the bottom of your soul and listen to God there?

6. How are you practicing self-examination and confession these days? Where are you experiencing increasing freedom from your false-self patterns? Where do you sense God inviting you to greater freedom?

7. How are your sacred rhythms resulting in an increasing capacity to be available to God for others? Reflect on a specific time when you saw this and knew it was true.

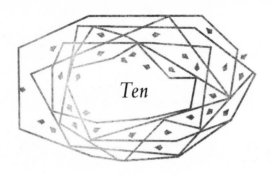

Ten

FINDING
SPIRITUAL FREEDOM

Where the Spirit of the Lord is, there is freedom.

2 CORINTHIANS 3:17

WHILE ON RETREAT, I WAS TAKEN BY SURPRISE when a spiritual director raised the issue of spiritual freedom as I talked about the unworkable nature of my life and its demands. In response to my despair, he began by stating that I needed to find my spiritual freedom. Tears immediately sprang to my eyes, and whatever was causing them was so deep that I could find no words at all. The fact that there were only tears and no words alerted me that there was something here I needed to pay attention to.

It's not that I had never heard the words *spiritual freedom* strung together before, and it's not like I was unfamiliar with the verse "Where the Spirit of the Lord is, there is freedom." It's actually one of my favorites that I refer to often. No, my life has been characterized by such a strong sense of responsibility that the idea of spiritual freedom was a possibility I had never fully allowed myself to consider—at least not for myself. I realized I was not sure I had ever really felt free—especially from the many responsibilities that had always given shape to my existence. *How does one balance freedom and responsibility?* I wondered.

SOMETHING'S GOT TO GIVE

After waiting for my emotions to subside a little, my director followed up with the observation that I needed to allow my options to surface, without trying too hard. He suggested I explore the freedoms I *did* have and how I could exercise those more fully. Simply framing the question this way made me realize I had a lot of the freedom I was looking for but wasn't exercising it. *What was that all about?* I wondered.

Then he threw a small hand grenade into the middle of our conversation. He mentioned rather offhandedly that a strategy of the evil one is to use good things against us *and* to use our gifts against us. Sometimes our gifts are actually destroying us, and our gifts and strengths can undermine the greater good God is laboring to bring forth in our lives. It's a good thing I was on retreat because to get to the bottom of all *that* without trying too hard and then to *own* the answer would take time and the safety of a nonjudgmental attitude. My judging mind and overly responsible self was already putting up a fight!

The answer to the first question came rather quickly, and it's something I've known for a long time. One of the reasons I struggle to live consistently within rhythms that are good for me and that meet my heart's deepest desire is that I desperately do not want to disappoint the people I love and care about most. When my desire for God and a certain way of life is so different from what others want and expect, it is very hard. Now, I know some folks who don't seem to care if they disappoint others; they go blithely on their way, barely aware, it seems, that anyone is unhappy with them. I envy their emotional freedom.

For as long as I can remember I have not been able to tolerate knowing I have disappointed someone—especially the people I love most. I will do almost anything to avoid the feeling! Even though I've done a lot of work related to this, it's still a part of who I am, and when I am stuck in this personality pattern, I am not free.

When we find that we are not living in rhythms consistent with our heart's deepest desire, it can be helpful to ask, *Is this kind of power-lessness or unfreedom something that might be at work in my life? And can I say something honest to God about this?*

SPIRITUAL FREEDOM—WHAT?

Increasingly, it seems that many of us feel we don't have the freedom to order our lives within the sacred rhythms that will open us to intimacy with ourselves, with God, and with others. There is often an unexamined feeling of powerlessness in light of the forces of cultural expectation—be it the culture of our country, our ethnic and family culture, the professional culture related to our work, even the subculture in our town, neighborhood, or church.

We often feel powerlessness in the face of aspects of our personality as well. We each have an inner culture that is affected by our person-ality patterns, such as a relentless drive to succeed, to be perfect, to not disappoint others, or simply to avoid conflict. When we are at the mercy of these cultures, we are not free to recalibrate our lives as God leads and as our desire dictates. Allowing ourselves to become aware of these places of unfreedom is a step in the right direction.

To be clear, spiritual freedom is not the freedom to do anything I want. It is freedom from everything that is not God; it is being solely oriented and responsive to the person of Christ in the depths of our being. The Jesuit John English describes spiritual freedom this way:

> The freedom I am speaking about is a kind of realized, existential freedom—freedom with oneself, and freedom within oneself. It

might be called *ultimate freedom*, the freedom that accompanies deep awareness of the ultimate meaning of one's life. Ultimate freedom requires an acceptance of oneself as historically coming from God, going to God and being with God. It includes a sense of well-being, self-identity, and basic peace.

I knew I wanted *that* more than anything.

DISORDERED ATTACHMENT

Real insight came as I began to realize that this unfreedom was the result of a disordered attachment—a place where I cared more about what other people thought and felt than what God was inviting me to. And it was not just that my disordered attachment was to the people in my life, it was actually a disordered attachment *to my image of myself* in relation to people and their expectations.

Spiritual freedom is not the freedom to do anything I want. It is freedom from everything that is not God; it is being solely oriented and responsive to the person of Christ in the depths of our being.

I had this ideal in my head—this utterly grandiose belief—that somehow I could follow God without disappointing anyone. That I was so special I could do everything and be everything to everyone I cared about without ever disappointing them and without ever having to see in their eyes or hear in their voices that my choices made them sad. There was a bit of magical thinking going on too—that I was special enough that somehow I could transcend the limits of time, space, and humanness others have to live with. Ridiculous, I know, but there you have it.

Now we were getting to one of the real sources of my lack of freedom to live within the rhythms God was inviting me to, rhythms I know are good for body, mind, and soul. The real sources were my unwillingness to disappoint others, my inability to live with disappointment (my own and others'), an inordinate attachment to an idealized and unrealistic view of myself, plus some grandiosity thrown in. Spiritual freedom would be the freedom to be what and who God is calling me to be, not who I am determined to be or who others are expecting me to be.

Again, John English is helpful:

> Many people think that all attachments are disordered, but they are not. There are attachments that are ordered to the end for which they were created. They bring us closer to God and to other people. The problem is not with ordered attachments; it is with disordered attachment. Disordered attachments turn us in on ourselves; they are strictly concerned with self. This self-concern is expressed when we are selfish or too other-centered. They are enslaving. They chain us and prevent us from being free with ourselves, free with other human beings, and free in the whole context of life.

QUESTIONS THAT HAVE NO RIGHT TO GO AWAY

As I began to see these disordered attachments for what they were, I opened myself to a new set of questions: What is God showing me that I can freely let go of so I can live the rhythms and patterns he is calling me to? How do I feel when I offer this to the Lord? Can I walk around as if I were letting go of this thing and see how it feels deep inside (consolation or desolation)?

A regular practice of retreat helps us find a still point from which to take stock of our days and decisions. Does the way I am living day to day correspond to the deepest desire of my heart? Am I ordering my days around the purposes God has for me, and saying the courageous noes that enable me to put first things first? What are those first things, and are there any changes that need to be made so I can live the life God has for me? Then we recalibrate so we can reenter our lives with a clearer sense of how God is leading us to live *in this current season*. In my experience, this kind of recalibration is always a part of retreat time.

All this reminds me of what happened at the end of Elijah's retreat into solitude in 1 Kings 19. After he had rested, after he had gotten quiet enough to say something honest to God about his life, after the chaos had settled, after he had encountered God in the depths of his being and basked in that presence for a while, God freely offered clear guidance for how to reenter his life in a healthier way. There were two aspects of this guidance—one strategic and one personal. The strategic aspect had to do with going back and appointing a new king, which Elijah did. The personal aspect had to do with the fact that the way Elijah was living was not sustainable, and so God told him to go back, find Elisha, and share the mantle of leadership with him rather than continuing to bear the mantle of leadership alone. This he also did, and that is what made his life sustainable until the chariot swung low and carried him home.

A regular practice of retreat helps us find a still point from which to take stock of our days and decisions.

So what is the guidance God is offering you? Do you have the courage to go home and follow it? In case you need help, I invite you to sink and settle into the interlude immediately following this chapter; it contains a poem I often carry with me into retreat to foster a sense of freedom and permission to live life on God's terms for me.

Practicing RETREAT

While on retreat. What is your greatest challenge to living in sacred rhythms? Is there any place of unfreedom you become aware of as you reflect on the way you are ordering your life these days?

How is God inviting you to greater *spiritual* freedom that emerges from "a deep awareness of the ultimate meaning of one's life and acceptance of oneself as coming from God, going to God, and being with God"?

With greater freedom, how might you recalibrate your life for the specific functions and purposes God has for you now?

Do you notice a sense of freedom or unfreedom as you consider this?

Note: It may take a while to find the inner quiet that makes it possible to be honest about whether you have found spiritual freedom or not. Let this question come to you as God brings it, and allow God to give you needed insight.

When you have some clarity about this, find a way to "own" it by writing about it in a journal, speaking about it directly to God, or naming it out loud to your spiritual director.

INTERLUDE

Sometimes

Sometimes
if you move carefully
through the forest,

breathing
like the ones
in the old stories,

who could cross
a shimmering bed of leaves
without a sound,

you come
to a place
whose only task

is to trouble you
with tiny
but frightening requests,

conceived out of nowhere
but in this place
beginning to lead everywhere.

Requests to stop what
you are doing right now,
and

to stop what you
are becoming
while you do it,

questions
that can make
or unmake
a life,

questions
that have patiently
waited for you,

questions
that have no right
to go away.

David Whyte, 2003

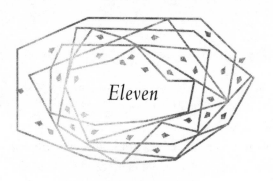

Eleven

REMEMBER
the SIGNS

Whatever the spiritual benefits of our retreat time,
we must always remember that these blessings are not only
for ourselves but for the sake of the communities we belong
to—our families, circles of friendship, our churches,
society at large. The experience of God pours
loving energy into us, qualifies us to serve
others with charm and delight.

EMILIE GRIFFIN

THERE IS A STORY IN THE CHRONICLES OF NARNIA that for me has always captured what it's like to think of returning from retreat to reengage in the life we share with others. In the opening chapter of *The Silver Chair* two school children, Jill and Scrubb, are fighting and tussling with each other too close to the edge of a cliff, and the boy, Scrubb, ends up tumbling over the precipice. Jill is devastated because she feels responsible for the debacle, even as she tries to rationalize her role in the whole thing. She cries for a while in utter despair, face down on the ground, but eventually gets up feeling thirsty. She hears a stream gurgling in the woods nearby and wants desperately to find it and take a drink. The only problem is that she had gotten a glimpse of a large lion in the vicinity and isn't sure if it's real or just a figment of her imagination.

Frightened but also driven by thirst, she heads toward the sound of the stream; lo and behold, the biggest lion she has ever seen is lying right there in front of it, head raised and alert, its two paws straight out in front of its body. She knows if she runs, the lion (who is also known as Aslan and is the Christ figure in the story) could easily catch her; if she heads toward the stream for a drink, she will run straight into its mouth. She stands frozen on the horns of quite a dilemma.

"If you are thirsty, you may drink," the Lion says.

"I am *dying* of thirst," says Jill.

"Then drink," says the Lion.

"May I—could I—would you mind going away while I do?" says Jill.

The Lion answers this with a low growl, convincing Jill she has no choice but to take the risk of approaching the stream; the delicious sound of running water is "driving her nearly frantic" with longing.

"Will you promise not to—do anything if I do come?" says Jill.

"I make no promise," says the Lion. Jill was so thirsty by now that, without realizing it, she had come a step nearer.

"Do you eat girls?" she asks.

"I have swallowed up girls and boys, women and men, kings and emperors, cities and realms," says the Lion, quite unapologetically.

"I daren't come and drink," says Jill.

"Then you will die of thirst," says the Lion.

"Oh dear," said Jill, coming another step nearer. "I suppose I must go and look for another stream then."

"There is no other stream," says the Lion.

Her mind suddenly made up, Jill does the worst thing she has ever had to do; she moves toward the stream, kneels down, and begins scooping up water in her hand. It is the coldest and most refreshing water she had ever tasted, and she discovers that one doesn't need to drink much of it, for it quenches your thirst at once. Before tasting it she had intended to make a mad dash away from the Lion the moment she was finished. Now she realizes this would be the most dangerous thing she could do. So she straightens up, lips still wet from drinking, ready to accept her fate.

THERE IS NO OTHER STREAM

This, to me, is what it feels like to come to the end of retreat time. We entered into retreat driven by desperate thirst: for God, for rest, for goodness, for more. (These days, that kind of desperation is about the only thing that would cause any of us to do something as radical as unplugging completely, leaving our life in the company of others, and seeking God in a way that threatens our normal mode of existence.) We've tried to find another stream—other ways to quench our thirst— but we have become pretty well convinced that approaching *this* stream *in this way* is our only hope for quenching such deep thirst. And on retreat, we drink—oh, how deeply we drink!—until we wonder how we ever survived without the cold, clear, refreshing water that has been so utterly satisfying. We have experienced something more than we ever thought possible. Now we are standing there, our lips still dripping with living water, wondering what we are supposed to do next.

In this story, the Lion initiates a conversation with Jill similar to what we might have experienced on retreat: he helps her process the less-than-stellar aspects of her personality that contributed to the mishap at the edge of the cliff. He gives her a chance to come clean about own her own false-self stuff in such a way that she knows all will be well. Scrubb is safe because the Lion has blown him to Narnia;

a load has been lifted and she is free from the burden of past mistakes. But there is responsibility as well. The Lion informs her that what she has experienced is more than just a private interlude. There is a task ahead, something that is being asked of her.

"Please, what task, Sir?" says Jill.

"The task for which I called you and him here out of your own world."

Jill is puzzled. *It's mistaking me for someone else*, she thinks. "I was wondering—I mean—could there be some mistake? Because nobody called me and Scrubb, you know. It was we who asked to come here. Scrubb said we were to call to—to Somebody—it was a name I wouldn't know—and perhaps Somebody would let us in. And we did, and then we found the door open."

"You would not have called me unless I had been calling you," the Lion responds.

"Then you are Somebody, Sir?" Jill asks.

"I am. And now hear your task."

The Lion describes the task ahead of her. He also describes four signs she is to watch for and tells her exactly what to do when she sees them. Then, before their encounter is complete, he instructs her about how to reengage her life:

> Remember, remember, remember the Signs. Say them to yourself when you wake in the morning and when you lie down at night, and when you wake in the middle of the night. And whatever strange things happen to you, let nothing turn your mind from following the signs. And secondly, I give you a warning. Here on the mountain I have spoken to you clearly; I will not often do so down in Narnia. Here on the mountain, the air is clear and your mind is clear; as you drop down into Narnia, the air will thicken. Take great care that it does not confuse your mind. And the Signs which you have learned here will not look at all like you expect them to look, when you meet them there. That is why

it is so important to know them by heart and pay no attention to appearances. Remember the Signs and believe the Signs. Nothing else matters. And now, Daughter of Eve, farewell.

REMEMBERING THE SIGNS

The purpose of retreat is always twofold: to become more deeply grounded in God as the ultimate orienting reality of our lives, and to return to the life God has given us with renewed strength, vitality, and clarity about how we are called to be in God for the world. The place we return to is our own Narnia. It is the place where Aslan is clearly on the move—involved in the affairs of humankind—but where the kingdom of God has not yet fully come and where the presence of God is harder to discern. Our prayer is that we might return as those who are increasingly responsive to God's presence—which we have come to experience more fully.

Understandably there might be some ambivalence about returning to life as we know it. While we might be missing our familiar life in the company of others, we also might have experienced such deep rest and communion with God, such clarity about what he is saying to us and how he is calling us, that we are actually afraid to go back for fear we cannot sustain the communion or hold on to the clarity we have received. We might experience a slight sense of dread that all the goodness and sustenance we have taken in on retreat might slip away, leaving us empty and disillusioned once again. We too must "remember the Signs" and capture as clearly as possible what God has

The purpose of retreat is always twofold: to become more deeply grounded in God as the ultimate orienting reality of our lives, and to return to the life God has given us with renewed strength, vitality, and clarity about how we are called to be in God for the world.

said to us so we can remember even when the air seems thick and the static grows louder in our ordinary lives.

Taking some time to journal around the following questions *before we leave* can help us to get clear on what God has said and done, and to claim it as our call going forward.

- What has God said to you on retreat that seems to be clear?

- What signs has God given you while on retreat to help you remember that the encounter you have had is real?

- Is there anything you can take with you as a token, a remembrance, of what you have experienced so that even in the thick of life you won't forget?

- Is there anything you will be watching for back at home, and what will you do when you see it?

Writing our responses to at least some of the questions can give us something to return to when the air thickens and we are having a hard time remembering that something real did happen—that God really did speak to us—while we were on retreat.

PREPARING FOR REENTRY

Seasoned retreat guides know that people must make some practical preparations for reentry; otherwise, they risk doing damage to themselves and to others. Just like a diver who comes up from the depths too quickly might experience decompression sickness (the bends) if they don't do decompression stops, a person who reenters normal life too quickly, ill-advisedly, or without making adequate preparations will be surprised at the shock to their system this can be.

Everyone responds differently to reengaging after retreat; some come home anxious to share their retreat experience, and others find that what took place for them is literally too deep for words. To complicate matters even further, what we want from the people we are returning to may be different from what they are capable of giving. For instance, one mother of teenagers knows that as eager as she might be to share, she will not be greeted with three children eager to listen to her experiences. "They usually say something like 'Where have you been?' 'Have you seen my red pants?' 'You can't believe what so-and-so did while you were away!' 'What's for dinner?'" she laughs. She has learned to take this in stride by being realistic about her life and rightsizing her expectations. Her prayer as she returns is that she will be able to be present to her family and their concerns with the same kind of presence God has given to her on retreat.

Or as this man shares, "My problem is the exact opposite. Our children are grown and gone, and my wife is very interested in my spiritual journey. She will want to hear all about it, and I will have trouble finding words. She used to think I was withholding things from her, and she felt left out. Now she understands that it may take days before I am able to share." His prayer as he makes his way home might be that God would give him a few words to offer when he gets home, along with the understanding that more will come later. While acknowledging the limits of his ability to communicate fully about what he has experienced, he might even purchase a book that became important to him while he was on retreat and share it as a way of connecting his wife with the experience, or he might bring home a candle, an icon, or a religious symbol that could be a way to share what he would like to share with her. A person who comes home from retreat bearing gifts is always appreciated!

As parents of young children return from retreat, they might become aware of how hard their spouse has worked to make their retreat possible. The retreatant might allow their heart to fill with gratitude for the gift of having been on retreat, and determine to give generously in ways that are meaningful to the other as they return. They might ponder, *What gifts can I bring to my loved ones who have missed me, the ones who have sacrificed, who have given of themselves to make this time away possible?* Because we have been given so much on retreat, now would be the time to think

Generosity of spirit is the key as we return from retreat.

about what others might need—a time for us to listen to what they experienced while we were gone, a date night, or an evening out with a friend. Generosity of spirit is the key as we return.

BE KIND TO YOURSELF AND EVERYONE ELSE!

We need to remember also that most of us return from retreat feeling open and vulnerable, and highly sensitive to the too-muchness of life with others—too much noise, too much activity, too many demands. Having been to the mountaintop, we might imagine through rose-colored glasses that reentry will be an unequivocally blessed thing and then be crushed when it doesn't live up to our expectations. Perfect reunions rarely happen. As one young mother confessed, "I walked into the house full of love and gratitude for my family, took one look at the messy kitchen, and yelled at my kids for being irresponsible and my husband for not doing things the way I would have done them."

Whatever our reality is, it must be graciously accepted; it is wise to be realistic and prepared. The people you are retuning to have not been where you've been, so don't expect them to be where you are. If you can make your return to normal life a little bit gradual, that will be helpful. Create realistic expectations for when your family might expect to hear from you and when you will walk in the door following your retreat so you can be relaxed heading home. If you are driving, leave the radio off and use the drive as a part of easing back in. If you had your phone turned off while on retreat (which I hope you did!), wait until you feel ready to turn it back on and maybe only listen to a few messages at time. If you are taking a flight home, use

the time at the airport for final journaling and preparations to reengage. So you are prepared, call home and get a bead on what happened while you were gone and what you are walking into. Make
opening up email the last thing you do after you have settled back
in and gotten your equilibrium.

*Do not, under any circumstances, let yourself get lured into saying more
about your retreat than you are ready to say or share spiritual things with
people who are not ready or able to receive it.* Tell people something, but
don't tell them more than you are ready to tell or they are ready to
receive. This is a loving choice all the way around.

As Jane Vennard so wisely cautions, "The way up from the depths
is as important as the way down the mountain. We cannot expect to
simply return to the familiar and be ready for it."

Practicing RETREAT

Preparing to head home. Just as you prepared to go on retreat, now take time to prepare for reentry. Before heading back to your life in the company of others, take time to reflect prayerfully on the following questions; record in your journal what God says to you so you can "remember the Signs" and solidify your own intentions:

~ What has God said to you on retreat that seems to be clear? What signs has he given you to help you remember that what he has said to is real, even in the thick of life in our culture and in the company of others? What will you be watching for?

~ Reflect on what you will encounter as you reenter. Who and what is waiting for you as you return home? Which of these are you looking forward to? Which do feel reluctant about encountering? Talk to God about these. Listen for his response and his specific guidance for how to face each one.

~ What gifts has God given you to share with others as you return?

~ How can you be wise and even protective of your tender, exposed self—the self that has become so safe, open, and vulnerable in God's presence and in the safety of the retreat environment? Ask, How can I return, being sensitive to myself *and* to others?

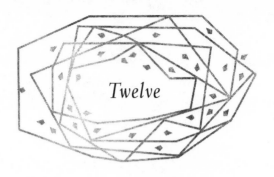

Twelve

In RETURNING *and* REST YOU SHALL BE SAVED

Therefore, the LORD *waits to be gracious to you.*

ISAIAH 30:18

T HERE IS THIS WONDERFUL DOUBLE ENTENDRE contained within the invitation to return—there is the invitation to return to our lives *and* the invitation to return to God through a regular practice of retreat. So if you would, take out your Bible and turn to Isaiah 30. Verse 15 describes a God who is always waiting for us to return to a place of rest in him, even though everything outside us clamors to keep us distracted rather than grounded in God. This great verse is often taken out of context, but it's even better when read in context. So read the whole chapter and see if you resonate with the author's description of God's willful people who literally run the other way when God is calling them to himself—to rest, to trust, and to take their cues from the voice of their teacher, who is trying to guide them, saying, "This is the way; walk in it" (v. 21). Do you see yourself in this description? I know I do!

Like the rebellious people God describes so poignantly in this passage, the truth is *we* are the people who carry out a plan that is not from God. *We* make alliances and partnerships that may or may not be God's best plan for us. *We* go down to Egypt—back to the place where we were in bondage—seeking security there. *We* orient our lives around the acquisition of wealth rather than the cultivation of substance, seeking easier answers than those found in God's presence on retreat. *We* avoid truth by saying to the wise ones among us,

"Do not see,"
  and to the prophets, "Do not prophesy to us what is right;
speak to us the smooth things,
    prophesy illusions,
leave the way, turn aside from the path,
    let us hear no more about the Holy One of Israel."
      (vv. 10-12)

We run the other way—not on horses, perhaps, but in cars and on airplanes—when the Holy One is calling us to be still in God's presence. Oh Lord, make haste to help us!

I don't know about you, but I need to be saved every day. From life in our culture, yes, and from the forces of evil in the world. But mostly I need to be saved from myself—from my own busyness and the weariness that comes with it. From my feelings of self-importance. From grabbing at things that aren't being given. From micromanaging what I have been given. From my relentless human striving. From the anger and bitterness and cynicism that threaten to take over when I have not had the chance to tell God the truth of my heart and allowed God to address me in that place.

In returning and rest you shall be saved.

A PLACE TO RETURN TO

In Old Testament times, there were certain geographical places where God was known to show up. Since retreat is an extended time in solitude in which we are present to God and God alone, there are places described in Scripture that could rightly be identified as retreat centers! One such place was Horeb, the mountain of God, which was also known as Mount Sinai. This was one of Israel's most significant meeting places with God, and many good things happened there. This is where Moses met God routinely as a friend meets with a friend. It's where he received the Ten Commandments, where the presence of God passed by at Moses' request, and where he and God argued it out when they needed to. This is where Elijah had his famous, life-altering encounter with God as well.

Because God had consistently shown up in this particular place throughout Israel's history, it became a spiritual destination—a place God seekers returned to again and again when they needed an encounter with the living God. There were no guarantees (because none of us have God in our back pocket), but when someone was serious about finding God, Mount Horeb was a good bet. It was what we might today call a thin place—a place where heaven and earth seem very close and the veil between the two is very thin. So my question is, do you have such a place?

I ask this question because I think it is possible for modern-day seekers to identify places like this. I am not talking about the local Starbucks, which most likely is busy and crowded, and where everyone is scrolling through text messages and pecking at their keyboards. I am talking about places like a retreat center, a hermitage, a cottage on a lake, a bench in a park, a cell in a monastery, or a corner of a chapel—a place where the very act of returning there helps us retreat and rest ourselves in God. It might be a community of people (like a monastic community or a praying community in a retreat setting) who gather in a particular way with particular rhythms of prayer and silence that support our spiritual seeking. *The only criterion for retreat is that it be a place where you can enter into silence and are supported in the silence.* For this reason alone, I do not suggest a hotel or a conference center, because such an environment leaves us open to noise, music, television and other technology, and chatty staff. Being silent when everyone around us is talking and all the technologies are available is just too hard; there is simply too much temptation.

The only criterion for retreat is that it be a place where you can enter into silence and are supported in the silence.

These days, especially, we need support for our silence—either from a community that is holding silence together or from a place that is designed for this. One of the most blessed phrases I have read on materials sent ahead of a retreat is, "The house will be in silence when you arrive." The first time I read that statement, I thought, *If I can just crawl my way to that silence, I will be okay.* I have come to realize that silence is what makes a retreat a retreat. Whatever I have done to get away and put distance between myself and the battle line is only the beginning; it is entering into the silence that lets me know I have arrived someplace different. And staying in the silence creates space for God to do what only God knows needs to be done in my life.

Once we have identified a place we can return to, we can make our travel there a kind of pilgrimage in which we set out on a risky adventure for the express purpose of being available to God and meeting God in whatever unpredictable situations we may encounter along the way. Of course, this means we might consider unplugging from technology so that even as we travel we are starting to settle down and settle in, moving more at God's pace than the pace of our culture. This might seem radically countercultural today, but think about it—just a few short years ago, everyone traveled unplugged because being plugged in while traveling was impossible!

THE WILDERNESS WITHIN

Beyond physical destinations, the practice of retreat itself can become a place that helps us center ourselves in the presence of God and open ourselves to that presence. We might simply refer to this as *a space in time* that has been set aside for the sacred purpose of being present to God and God alone, a space in which we offer the great Lover of our souls our full and undivided attention. We can even retreat in place by closing our front door, shutting down our electronic devices for a period of time, and letting people know we are unavailable.

The practice of retreat means we are fashioning a *wilderness within* that is always available and we can always return to. "To live a spiritual life we must first find the courage to enter into the desert of our loneliness and to change it by gentle and persistent efforts into a garden of solitude." And

> *The practice of retreat means we are fashioning a wilderness within that is always available and we can always return to.*

there we find our retreat. However we do it, we are establishing rhythms that give us a concrete way of returning to God with all our heart, soul, mind, and strength.

I no longer see retreat as a self-indulgent luxury or as a rhythm that can wait for times when I am less busy. I see it as essential for long-term sustainability and life-sustaining connection with the One who enlivens my soul and empowers my service.

LIFTING POWER

What happens within us that makes it possible to return to our life in the company of others with ease and confidence? Here is a metaphor that helps describe what takes place on retreat:

> The main purpose of retreat is simply to be in the Presence. . . . The paramount aim is to have a period of uninterrupted closeness to God. Take this as an example. A ship enters a canal lock. It turns off its engines. The propellers stop. The canal doors are shut. The vessel just sits there. As the new level of water flows in, everything is lifted. When the doors open, the boat goes out at a new altitude, buoyed up not by anything it has done, but by the lifting power all around it.

This "lifting power" is what I have experienced over and over again on retreat. After years of practicing this key Christian discipline, I know that when I don't enter the lock at regular intervals, my life will just keep sinking to the level of the culture around me and to the level of my own unexamined inner world. However, when I enter the lock that is retreat, when I allow the doors to close behind me and wait quietly for my soul to be lifted by the presence of God, I find that almost imperceptibly I am buoyed to new levels. When I emerge I may not be able to say exactly what happened, but I know I have been lifted to new heights and my sails are straight and ready to catch the wind of the Spirit as it blows through my life. There is simply no substitute for this. Nothing I could do for myself even approaches *what God can do for me* in the context of retreat.

When I trust that good things have happened on retreat that I might not even be aware of—that I have been lifted to a higher plane just by being in God's presence—I am ready to return. I trust good things will come to me and to others, and this is how we will all be saved.

Practicing RETREAT

As you conclude your retreat. What is your experience now of the truth "in returning and rest you shall be saved"? What do you need to be saved from?

How is God inviting you to incorporate regular rhythms of returning and rest? (Pull out your calendar and identify when you will next return.)

Ask God to show you what typically keeps you from saying yes to his invitation, and determine to meet your avoidance tactics head-on!

GRATITUDES

THIS BOOK WAS A HARD ONE TO FINISH, given that life kept happening. While this book was trying to find its way into the world, perhaps the most significant life happening was that I had the privilege of caring for my mother and walking closely with her during her final days. It was a sacred journey, and I have no regrets—except that I will not be able to take a copy of the finished product straight to her when it comes out, as I have always done. I learned so much from her about letting go into God as she made her final journey—which is not unlike going on a retreat. I dedicate this book to her in hopes that I can let go as gracefully as she did when my time comes.

I am grateful to my long-time editor, Cindy Bunch, who was infinitely patient as she watched things happen in my life that could not be controlled, which required my presence and attention and kept me from writing. If I had had an editor who held a hard line on deadlines, I might have collapsed in a heap. But instead I have written a book—better late than never.

The Transforming Center continues to be my transforming community —a community that practices together and stays together. The teachings and practices contained in this book were developed and honed in the context of our life and practice—especially the practice of retreat. I thank God for you! Special thanks go to Dalene Strieff, who holds my professional life together, who walks with me in a discerning way, and who somehow keeps thinking it's all worth it. She (and we) lost her husband, David, during the writing of this book as well, and we miss him every day.

And to my family. Retreat is a hard thing because it means I have to leave you, which I never want to do. But I always come back better— and for that I am grateful, because my deepest desire is to give you my best self. To my long-suffering husband, Christopher; my loving daughters and their dear husbands—Charity and Kyle, Bethany and Ryan, Haley and Troy; and my beautiful grandchildren, thank you for letting me go and always welcoming me back.

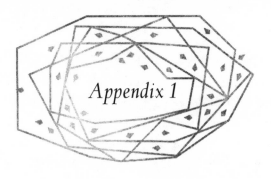

Appendix 1

FIXED-HOUR PRAYER

THERE ARE MANY WONDERFUL RESOURCES to help us pray the hours while we are on retreat. Phyllis Tickle has produced a three-volume prayer manual titled *The Divine Hours*. It is a liturgical reworking of the sixth-century Benedictine Rule of fixed-hour prayer, which includes one volume for summer, one for autumn and winter, and one for spring. These are thick volumes, so they are best used at home. There is also a pocket edition available, which is easier carry.

Several prayer books are useful due to their simplicity and their portable size. One is *Hour by Hour*, an Anglican prayer book based solely on Scripture and the Book of Common Prayer. Another is the *Book of Little Hours*, which emerged out of the shared life of the Community of Jesus, an ecumenical Christian community in the Benedictine tradition. These slim volumes are easy to travel with and share with others. The Book of Common Prayer is a wonderful resource as well, but to use it well, some orientation is needed.

Shane Claiborne, Jonathan Wilson-Hartgrove, and Enuma Okoro have offered *Common Prayer: A Liturgy for Ordinary Radicals*, which is oriented toward themes of justice. It highlights saints and others who have championed racial justice, compassion, and ministry to the poor and outcasts. Another resource I highly recommend to take on retreat is *A Guide to Prayer*, published by the Upper Room. There are several versions—one for "ministers and other servants," one for "all God's people," and one for "all who wait for God." These include retreat schedules by theme; other suggestions for retreat use are found in the back. I recommend them all!

I am also including a sampling of the simple fixed-hour prayers we have put together in the Transforming Center. Since I suggest starting retreat in the evening, if possible, I will start with a night prayer that helps us enter into rest and conclude with evening prayer the next day. Because we pray as a community, I have left them as communal expressions.

Even if you do not have a community to pray with, the "us" and "we" language can help keep you in touch with the communion of saints and the cascade of prayers being offered around the world—of which you are a part. I have also included Scriptures, but feel free to use lectionary Scriptures if you are following a shared lectionary or any other schedule of readings you have chosen for retreat. If you are praying alone, you might find it meaningful to read the Psalms and Scriptures out loud. If candles are allowed, lighting a candle can be a concrete reminder of the real presence of Christ mediated through the Holy Spirit. If you are praying with others, the upper- and lowercase lines are for the leader, and the all uppercase lines are for everyone to read together. If you are praying alone, you will read/pray all the words.

A LITURGY FOR NIGHT PRAYER

(before retiring)

OPENING

Our shouts greet you, Shepherd God.
WE HAVE BEEN LED BY YOUR LOVING HAND,
AND WE PROCLAIM WITH JOY THAT YOU
ARE OUR SALVATION.
Reign in our hearts this night.
AMEN.

CANDLE LIGHTING

NIGHT PRAYER

May God grant us a quiet night and peace at the last.
AMEN.

It is good to give thanks to the Lord,
TO SING PRAISE TO YOUR NAME, O MOST HIGH;
To herald your love in the morning,
YOUR TRUTH AT THE CLOSE OF THE DAY.

PSALM 31

LEADER   In you, O Lord, I seek refuge; do not let me ever be
           put to shame; in your righteousness deliver me.

RESPONSE   Incline your ear to me; rescue me speedily. Be a rock
           of refuge for me, a strong fortress to save me.

LEADER   You are indeed my rock and my fortress; for your
           name's sake lead me and guide me, take me out of
           the net that is hidden for me, for you are my refuge.

RESPONSE   Into your hand I commit my spirit; you have
           redeemed me, O Lord, faithful God.

PSALM PRAYER

You *have* redeemed me, O Lord, God of truth.
HEAR MY PRAYER, O LORD; LISTEN TO MY CRY.
Keep me as the apple of your eye;
HIDE ME IN THE SHADOW OF YOUR WINGS.
In righteousness I shall see you;
WHEN I AWAKE, YOUR PRESENCE WILL GIVE ME JOY.

READING FROM SCRIPTURE

Read Mark 6:30-51
(After the reading)
This is the Word of the Lord!
THANKS BE TO GOD.

Invitation to Rest

O Holy God, open unto us light for our darkness, courage for our fear, hope for our despair.

O LOVING GOD, OPEN UNTO US WISDOM FOR OUR CONFUSION, FORGIVENESS FOR OUR SINS, LOVE FOR OUR HATE.

O God of Peace, open unto us peace for our turmoil, joy for our sorrow, strength for our weakness.

O GENEROUS GOD, OPEN OUR HEARTS TO RECEIVE ALL YOUR GIFTS.

AMEN.

Silence

Let us release our burdens in silence to God.

The Lord's Prayer

As Jesus taught us, so we pray:
OUR FATHER IN HEAVEN,
HALLOWED BE YOUR NAME,
YOUR KINGDOM COME, YOUR WILL BE DONE,
ON EARTH AS IN HEAVEN.
GIVE US TODAY OUR DAILY BREAD.
FORGIVE US OUR SINS AS WE FORGIVE THOSE
WHO SIN AGAINST US.
SAVE US FROM THE TIME OF TRIAL,
AND DELIVER US FROM EVIL.
FOR THE KINGDOM, THE POWER, AND THE GLORY
ARE YOURS
NOW AND FOR EVER.
AMEN.

Canticle of Simeon

Lord, you now have set your servants free
To go in peace as you have promised;
FOR THESE EYES OF MINE HAVE SEEN THE SAVIOR,

WHOM YOU HAVE PREPARED FOR ALL THE WORLD
TO SEE:
A LIGHT TO ENLIGHTEN THE NATIONS,
AND THE GLORY OF YOUR PEOPLE ISRAEL.

Dismissal and Blessing

Guide us waking, O God, and guard us sleeping;
that awake we may watch with Christ,
and asleep we may rest in Christ's peace.
Let us bless the Lord.
THANKS BE TO GOD.
The almighty and merciful God bless us and keep us.
AMEN.

A LITURGY FOR MORNING PRAYER
(before breakfast)

Opening

O God, open our lips,
AND WE SHALL DECLARE YOUR PRAISE. (Psalm 51:15)
God said: Let there be light; and there was light.
And God saw that the light was good. This very day the Lord
has acted!
LET US REJOICE!
Praise the Lord!
GOD'S NAME BE PRAISED!

Candle Lighting

Prayer

New every morning is your love, great God of light,
AND ALL DAY LONG YOU ARE WORKING FOR GOOD IN
THE WORLD.
STIR UP IN US DESIRE TO SERVE YOU, TO LIVE PEACE-
FULLY WITH OUR NEIGHBORS,

AND TO DEVOTE THIS DAY TO YOUR SON, OUR SAVIOR,
JESUS CHRIST THE LORD. AMEN.

Psalm 121

I lift up my eyes to the hills—from where will my help come?
MY HELP COMES FROM THE LORD, WHO MADE
HEAVEN AND EARTH.
He will not let your foot be moved; he who keeps you
will not slumber.
HE WHO KEEPS ISRAEL WILL NEITHER SLUMBER NOR
SLEEP.
The Lord is your keeper; the Lord is your shade at your
right hand.
THE SUN SHALL NOT STRIKE YOU BY DAY, NOR THE
MOON BY NIGHT.
The Lord will keep you from all evil; he will keep your life
THE LORD WILL KEEP YOUR GOING OUT AND YOUR
COMING IN
FROM THIS TIME ON AND FOREVERMORE

Psalm Prayer

Let us pray together.
WE PRAISE YOU WITH JOY, LOVING GOD,
FOR YOUR GRACE IS BETTER THAN LIFE ITSELF.
YOU HAVE SUSTAINED US THROUGH THE DARKNESS;
AND YOU BLESS US WITH LIFE IN THIS NEW DAY.
IN THE SHADOW OF YOUR WINGS WE SING FOR JOY
AND BLESS YOUR HOLY NAME. AMEN.

Reading from Scripture

Read Lamentations 3:22-33
(After the reading)
This is the Word of the Lord!
THANKS BE TO GOD.

Silence

Canticle of Zachariah (Luke 1:68-79)

LEADER   Blessed be the Lord, the God of Israel;
           he has come to his people and set them free.

RESPONSE   He has raised up for us a mighty Savior,
           born of the house of his servant David.

LEADER   He promised to show mercy to our fathers
           and to remember his holy covenant.

RESPONSE   This was the oath he swore to our father Abraham:
           to set us free from the hands of our enemies,
           free to worship him without fear,
           holy and righteous in his sight all the days
           of our life.

LEADER   And you, child, will be called the prophet of the
           Most High, for you will go before the Lord to
           prepare his ways,

RESPONSE   to give knowledge of salvation to his people by the
           forgiveness of their sins.

LEADER   By the tender mercy of our God, the dawn from on
           high will break upon us,

RESPONSE   to give light to those who sit in darkness and in
           the shadow of death and to guide our feet
           into the way of peace.

The Lord's Prayer

We pray together as Jesus taught us:
OUR FATHER IN HEAVEN,
HALLOWED BE YOUR NAME,
YOUR KINGDOM COME,
YOUR WILL BE DONE,
ON EARTH AS IN HEAVEN.
GIVE US TODAY OUR DAILY BREAD.
FORGIVE US OUR SINS AS WE FORGIVE THOSE

WHO SIN AGAINST US.
SAVE US FROM THE TIME OF TRIAL,
AND DELIVER US FROM EVIL.
FOR THE KINGDOM, THE POWER, AND THE GLORY
ARE YOURS
NOW AND FOR EVER.
AMEN.

BENEDICTION

Go forth into this day with the strong name of Jesus Christ to
sustain you.
THE GRACE OF OUR LORD JESUS CHRIST BE WITH US
ALL.
AMEN.

A LITURGY FOR MIDDAY PRAYER
(Before or after lunch)

OPENING

O God, make speed to save us.
O LORD, MAKE HASTE TO HELP US.

CANDLE LIGHTING

A GENERAL THANKSGIVING

LEADER	Almighty God, we give you thanks for this life and all its blessings,
RESPONSE	for joys great and simple, for gifts and powers more than we deserve,
LEADER	for love at the heart of your purpose and wisdom in all your works,
RESPONSE	for light in the world brought once in Christ and always shining through your Spirit.
LEADER	Giving thanks to you we pray for that light to dawn upon us daily

RESPONSE that we may always have grateful hearts,
          and a will to love and to serve you
          to the end of our days.

ALL   Hear our prayer and our praises,
          through Jesus Christ our Lord.

Amen.

PSALM READING—PSALM 131

O LORD, my heart is not lifted up,
my eyes are not raised too high;
I DO NOT OCCUPY MYSELF WITH THINGS
TOO GREAT AND TOO MARVELOUS FOR ME.
But I have calmed and quieted my soul,
like a weaned child with its mother;
MY SOUL IS LIKE A WEANED CHILD WITHIN ME.
O Israel, hope in the Lord
FROM THIS TIME ON AND FOREVERMORE.

READING FROM SCRIPTURE

Read Isaiah 30:15-21
(After the reading)
This is the Word of the Lord!
THANKS BE TO GOD.

SILENCE

PRAYER OF QUIET TRUST

Oh God of peace,
who has taught us that in returning and rest
we shall be saved,
in quietness and trust shall be our strength:
BY THE POWER OF YOUR HOLY SPIRIT
QUIET OUR HEARTS, WE PRAY,

SO THAT WE MAY BE STILL AND KNOW THAT
YOU ARE GOD,
THROUGH JESUS CHRIST OUR LORD.
AMEN.

The Lord's Prayer

We pray together as Jesus taught us:
OUR FATHER IN HEAVEN,
HALLOWED BE YOUR NAME,
YOUR KINGDOM COME,
YOUR WILL BE DONE,
ON EARTH AS IN HEAVEN.
GIVE US TODAY OUR DAILY BREAD.
FORGIVE US OUR SINS AS WE FORGIVE THOSE
WHO SIN AGAINST US.
SAVE US FROM THE TIME OF TRIAL,
AND DELIVER US FROM EVIL.
FOR THE KINGDOM, THE POWER, AND THE GLORY
ARE YOURS
NOW AND FOR EVER.
AMEN.

Dismissal

Let us go forth in the peace of Christ.
AMEN.
Let us bless the Lord.
THANKS BE TO GOD.

A LITURGY FOR EVENING PRAYER
(before dinner)

Opening

From the rising of the sun to its setting,
Let the name of the Lord be praised.
YOU, O LORD, ARE MY LAMP.
MY GOD, YOU MAKE MY DARKNESS BRIGHT.

Light and peace in Jesus Christ our Lord.
THANKS BE TO GOD.

CANDLE LIGHTING

EVENING PRAYER

We praise and thank you, O God,
FOR YOU ARE WITHOUT BEGINNING AND WITHOUT
END.
Through Christ, you created the whole world;
THROUGH CHRIST, YOU PRESERVE IT.
Through Christ you made the day for the works of light
AND THE NIGHT FOR THE REFRESHMENT OF OUR
MINDS AND OUR BODIES.
Keep us now in Christ, grant us a peaceful evening.
A NIGHT FREE FROM SIN, AND BRING US AT LAST
TO ETERNAL LIFE.
Through Christ and in the Holy Spirit,
WE OFFER YOU ALL GLORY, HONOR, AND WORSHIP,
NOW AND FOREVER. AMEN.

PSALM READING—PSALM 27

LEADER   The LORD is my light and my salvation;
             whom shall I fear?

RESPONSE   The LORD is the stronghold of my life;
             of whom shall I be afraid?

LEADER   When evildoers assail me to devour my flesh—
             my adversaries and foes—they shall
             stumble and fall.

RESPONSE   Though an army encamp against me,
             my heart shall not fear; though war rise up
             against me, yet I will be confident.

LEADER   One thing I asked of the LORD, that will I seek after:

RESPONSE   to live in the house of the LORD
all the days of my life,
to behold the beauty of the LORD,
and to inquire in his temple.

LEADER   For he will hide me in his shelter
in the day of trouble;
he will conceal me under the cover of his tent;
he will set me high on a rock.

RESPONSE   Now my head is lifted up above my enemies
all around me, and I will offer in his tent
sacrifices with shouts of joy;
I will sing and make melody to the LORD.

LEADER   Hear, O LORD, when I cry aloud,
be gracious to me and answer me!

RESPONSE   *"Come," my heart says, "seek his face!"*
Your face, LORD, do I seek.

LEADER   I believe that I shall see the goodness of the LORD
in the land of the living.

RESPONSE   Wait for the LORD; be strong, and let your heart take
courage;
wait for the LORD!
Amen.

PSALM PRAYER

Sovereign God, you have been our help during
the day and you promise to be with us at night.

RECEIVE THIS PRAYER AS A SIGN OF OUR TRUST
IN YOU.

SAVE US FROM ALL EVIL, KEEP US FROM HARM,

AND GUIDE US IN YOUR WAY. WE BELONG TO YOU,
LORD.

PROTECT US BY THE POWER OF YOUR NAME,

In Jesus Christ, we pray. AMEN.

Reading from Scripture

Read Mark 10:46-52

(After the reading)

This is the Word of the Lord!

THANKS BE TO GOD

Silence

Prayers of Intercession

(... indicates a brief silent pause)

Lord, in your mercy.

HEAR OUR PRAYER.

For the peace of the world, that a spirit of respect and forbearance may grow among nations and peoples ...

Lord, in your mercy. HEAR OUR PRAYER.

For the holy church of God, that it may be filled with truth and love, and be found without fault at the day of your coming ...

Lord, in your mercy. HEAR OUR PRAYER.

For those in positions of public trust, especially our president and congressional leaders, that they may serve justice and promote the dignity and freedom of all people ...

Lord, in your mercy. HEAR OUR PRAYER.

For a blessing upon the labors of all, and for the right use of the riches of creation ...

Lord, in your mercy. HEAR OUR PRAYER.

For the poor, the persecuted, the sick, and all who suffer; for refugees, prisoners, and all who are in danger: that they may be relieved and protected ...

Lord, in your mercy. HEAR OUR PRAYER.

For this community; for those who are present, and for those who are absent, that we may be delivered from hardness of heart, and may show forth your glory in all that we do ...

Lord, in your mercy. HEAR OUR PRAYER.

For our enemies and those who wish us harm; and for all whom we have injured or offended ...

Lord, in your mercy. HEAR OUR PRAYER.

For ourselves, for the forgiveness of our sins, and for the grace of the Holy Spirit to amend our lives ...

Lord, in your mercy. HEAR OUR PRAYER.

For all who commended themselves to our prayers: for our families, friends, and neighbors, that being freed from anxiety, they may live in joy, peace, and health ...

Lord, in your mercy. HEAR OUR PRAYER.

(Pause for bringing personal petitions before the Lord)

In the communion of the Holy Spirit and of all the saints,

let us commend ourselves and one another to the living God through Christ our Lord. AMEN.

MEALTIME BLESSING

Lord Jesus, stay with us

For evening is at hand and the day is past.

Be our companion in the way, and awaken hope

As you are revealed in Scripture and in the breaking of bread.

We ask this for the sake of your love.

AMEN.

BENEDICTION

Eternal Creator of light,

Yours is the morning and yours is the evening.

Draw us to yourself so there will be no darkness within us.

AMEN.

Let us go in peace.

THANKS BE TO GOD.

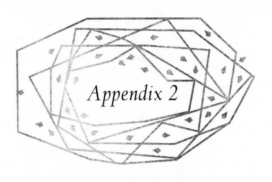

Appendix 2

PLANNING
YOUR RETREAT

TYPES OF RETREAT

- **Silent retreat.** A silent retreat entails complete silence at a retreat center or hermitage. See "Planning Your Own Retreat" for guidance on planning a silent retreat.

- **Private directed retreat.** A private directed retreat is a silent retreat with spiritual direction, which means you will meet regularly with a spiritual director, who will help give direction for your retreat based on what you need or what you are bringing. The director will also meet regularly with you throughout your retreat to listen with you what God is saying, support you in responding faithfully, and giving you further guidance as needed.

- **Preached retreat.** A preached retreat is taken with others and is led by a teacher or a retreat guide who offers meditations (often on a theme) and guidance throughout. It might be a retreat with people you know or a community you are a part of (like your church), or you might attend a retreat where you don't know anyone else but trust the person or the retreat center that is offering the retreat. Even though retreat guidance is given to a group and there may be some conversation in the group times, the atmosphere is still one of silence at meals and in the retreat facility for a good portion of the experience. The best preparation for a preached retreat is to enter with a posture of openness to God and a willingness to be guided by the person leading the retreat.

PLANNING YOUR OWN RETREAT

- Choose a retreat center, hermitage, or some other location that will make it possible for you to be in silence and experience the rest of God. Make a reservation. Find out what is offered so you can join in the life of that community or make plans yourself for things like meals, fixed-hour prayer, spiritual direction, and so forth.

- Set your intention. The purpose of all retreats is to draw close to God. Is there any additional and more specific intention you want to set for this retreat or some more specific aspect of your spiritual life you want to cultivate or attend to? It might be to rest in God, to discern something in particular, to explore or renew your call, to explore an area of sin or negative patterns and get unstuck.

- In addition to basic clothes and toiletries, think through what else you would like to have with you to support your experience: your own pillow if you need that to rest well, a journal, any spiritual reading that will support and catalyze the intention you've set, a prayer book if the community does not offer fixed-hour prayer, art supplies or writing papers if that is a part of how you connect with God, exercise bands or anything else you would like to have with you to stay active.

- Plan to unplug from technology and inform your family and work associates that you will be doing this. Give them the number where you will be staying so they can contact you in case of emergency. Decide before you go what you will do with your phone, computer, and other electronic devices.

SUGGESTED DAILY SCHEDULE

The following sample is not to be held rigidly; it simply suggests a bit of a structure. I will not give exact times because meal schedules will vary depending on where you are. There is a lot of open space in this schedule so you can take advantage of anything and everything the community has to offer that draws you into relationship with God and replenishes you—even if it stretches you or is outside your comfort zone. Options offered might be fixed-hour prayer, centering prayer, guided meditation, spiritual direction, an art class or time in an art studio, the Eucharist, a meditative walk or hike, yoga, stretching, massage, or other kinds of body work. Whatever you choose, *do it with God.*

- Silence upon waking—for simply being present to God; have an open and receptive posture. (If possible on retreat, sleep until you wake up and allow your body to tell you what it needs to catch up on sleep and become fully rested.)

- Shower and dress

- Morning prayer

- Breakfast

- A walk before or after breakfast

- Spiritual reading and journaling

- Spiritual direction, if available. Follow the guidance given.

- Midday prayer

- Lunch

- Nap

- Walking meditation or a more strenuous activity like a run, a hike, or working out with weights. (It is important to stay active and alert in your body while on retreat.)

- Spiritual reading, reflection on Scripture, journaling that might be more focused on the intention you have brought to retreat. Activities offered by the community—hopefully in silence.

- Evening prayer

- Dinner

- Reading for pleasure—poetry or a novel. Watch the sunset. Listen to music. An activity you would enjoy just for the pleasure of it.

- Prayerful reflection on what God has said to you today and how you are responding. Make notes or write in your journal to capture the insights and learnings of this day.

- Night prayer

- Bath or shower if that would help you relax

- To bed

NOTES

INTRODUCTION

4 *a generous commitment to our friendship with God*: Emilie Griffin, *Wilderness Time: A Guide for Spiritual Retreat* (New York: HarperSanFrancisco, 1997), 3.

5 *we yearn for more of God than our schedules will allow*: Griffin, *Wilderness Time*, 1.

   three images for reteat: These three images are described in Ron Rolheiser, "Creating Sabbath Space in Our Lives: A Video Retreat with Ron Rolheiser," Oblate Media and Communication, 2009.

1 STRATEGIC WITHDRAWAL

12 *Once the sheer impulse of life begins*: Ronald Rolheiser, *Sacred Fire: A Vision for a Deeper Human and Christian Maturity* (New York: Image, 2014), 6.

13 *A point may come on the spiritual journey*: Timothy M. Gallagher, *Spiritual Consolation: An Ignatian Guide for the Greater Discernment of Spirits* (New York: Crossroad, 2007), 23.

15 *like many addicts, I had sensed a personal crash coming*: Andrew Sullivan, "I Used to Be a Human Being," *New Yorker*, September 21, 2016, http://nymag.com/selectall/2016/09 /andrew-sullivan-my-distraction-sickness-and-yours.html.

16 *I began to realize*: Sullivan, "I Used to Be a Human Being."

    guided to info-nuggets: Sullivan, "I Used to Be a Human Being."

17 *crouched over their phones*: Sullivan, "I Used to Be a Human Being."

18 *I had never felt it*: Sullivan, "I Used to Be a Human Being."

    Over the next day, the feelings began to ebb: Sullivan, "I Used to Be a Human Being."

19 *verbal and visual noise*: Sullivan, "I Used to Be a Human Being."

    Sometimes I walk down the street: Sherry Turkle, *Alone Together: Why We Expect More from Technology and Less from Each Other* (New York: Pereus Books, 2011), 277.

20 *If the churches came to understand*: Sullivan, "I Used to Be a Human Being."

2 JUST FLOP DOWN

23 *When should I make a retreat?*: Emilie Griffin, *Wilderness Time: A Guide for Spiritual Retreat* (New York: HarperSanFrancisco, 1997), 17.

24 *the remedy for each one is different*: See Ruth Haley Barton, *Invitation to Solitude and Silence: Experiencing God's Transforming Presence* (Downers Grove, IL: InterVarsity Press, 2004).

26 *Excessive stress occurs*: Gabor Mate, *When the Body Says No: Exploring the Stress-Disease Connection* (Hoboken, NJ: John Wiley, 2003), 29.

27 *quiet lonely place*: Catherine Doherty, *Poustinia: Encountering God in Silence, Solitude and Prayer* (Combermere: ON: Madonna House, 1993), 14.

    In a dazed state: Doherty, *Poustinia*, 51.

3 THE SOURCES OF OUR EXHAUSTION

33 *poor emotional differentiation*: These ideas are an extreme simplification of one of the main tenants of family systems theory first described by Dr. Murray Bowen. This particular application is adapted from Roberta Gilbert, *Extraordinary Relationships: A New Way of Thinking About Human Interactions* (New York: John Wiley, 1992), 18-19.

35 *we will begin to disintegrate*: If you know you are carrying the burden of unhealed wounds or ungrieved grief, here are several resources that might help. You may even want to prepare for retreat by taking one of these with you: *Ambiguous Loss* by Pauline Boss; *Release: Healing from Wounds of Family, Church, and Community* (or anything) by Flora Slosson Wuellner; *Praying Through Our Losses* by Wayne Simsic; *Option B* by Sheryl Sandberg and Adam Grant; and *Healing Spiritual Wounds* by Carol Howard Merritt.

38 *Some of us need to discover*: Thomas Merton, *No Man Is an Island* (New York: Houghton Mifflin Harcourt, 1955), loc. 1451, Kindle.

4 FINDING YOUR RHYTHM ON RETREAT

46 *Kevin's story*: This story, including this quote from Henri Nouwen, was told by Kevin Kelly at Loyola House, Guelph, CA, August 5, 2016. Used by permission.

5 SWEET HOURS OF PRAYER

55 *Psalms were the Hebrew prayer book*: Scot McKnight, *Praying with the Church* (Brewster, MS: Paraclete Press, 2006), 31.

61 *When one prays the hours*: Phyllis Tickle, *Eastertide: Prayers for Lent Through Easter from the Divine Hours* (New York: Random House, 2004), xi-xii.

6 LETTING GO OF YOUR GRIP

65 *Making a retreat requires*: Emilie Griffin, *Wilderness Time: A Guide for Spiritual Retreat* (New York: HarperSanFrancisco, 1997), 25.

67 *In [his] absence*: Henri Nouwen, *The Living Reminder: Service and Prayer in Memory of Jesus Christ* (San Francisco: HarperSanFrancisco, 1997), 49.

68 *what Nouwen is specifically advocating*: Wil Hernandez, *Henri Nouwen and Spiritual Polarities: A Life of Tension* (New York: Paulist Press, 2012), 75.

7 RELINQUISHING FALSE-SELF PATTERNS

75 *Even lay down your ideas*: Dallas Willard, *The Divine Conspiracy: Rediscovering Our Hidden Life in God* (New York: HarperSanFrancisco, 1998), 359-60.

    to avoid relinquishing ourselves: For a helpful and concise treatment of these human programs for happiness and how they develop, see Thomas Keating, *The Human Condition: Contemplation and Transformation* (New York: Paulist Press, 1999).

76 *Enneagram nine patterns*: If you are not familiar with the Enneagram, there are many wonderful resources to consider: *The Enneagram: A Christian Perspective* by Richard Rohr and Andreas Ebert, *The Wisdom of the Enneagram* by Don Risso and Russ Hudson, *The Enneagram* by Helen Palmer, *The Road Back to You* by Ian Cron and Suzanne Stabile, *Mirror for the Soul* by Alice Fryling, just to name a few.

    the seven deadly sins: For more on this approach to greater self-awareness see *Signature Sins: Taming Our Wayward Hearts* by Michael Mangis, *Glittering Vices: A New Look at the Seven Deadly Sins and Their Remedies* by Rebecca Konyndyk DeYoung, and *I Told Me So: Self-Deception and the Christian Life* by Greg Ten Elshof.

    Everything is perfect: adapted from Marilyn Vancil, *Self to Lose, Self to Find* (Enumclaw, WA: Redemption Press, 2016), loc. 901, Kindle.

79 *nines seek to avoid everything*: Richard Rohr, *The Enneagram: A Christian Perspective* (New York: Crossroad, 2001), 184.

    It helps nines: Rohr, *Enneagram*, 193.

8 SPACE FOR DISCERNMENT

87 *cease striving*: The Hebrew word translated "be still" in Psalm 46:10 is *rapha*, which literally means "cease striving" or "let go of your grip." Psalm 46:10 can be an important verse for us while on retreat because it encourages us to cease striving and let God be God in our lives—especially as it relates to whatever we have brought into retreat time that is weighing on us.

92 *A point may come*: Timothy M. Gallagher, *Spiritual Consolation: An Ignatian Guide for the Greater Discernment of Spirits* (New York: Crossroad, 2007), 23, 38.

9 INVITATION TO RECALIBRATE

97 *Maybe my own deep-rooted*: Henri Nouwen, *Reaching Out: The Three Movements of the Spiritual Life* (New York: Doubleday, 1975), 14.

98 *Such a process involves*: see Ruth Haley Barton, *Sacred Rhythms: Arranging Our Lives for Spiritual Transformation* (Downers Grove, IL: InterVarsity Press, 2004). Retreat time is an excellent opportunity to explore different spiritual practices and then seek God's guidance for how you might arrange your life to incorporate them regularly.

99 *When we fail to distinguish*: Ronald Rolheiser, *Sacred Fire: A Vision for a Deeper Human and Christian Maturity* (New York: Random House, 2014), 9.

One example of such recalibration: Tom Kington, "Ex-Pope Benedict on Why He Resigned: 'God Told Me,'" *Los Angeles Times*, August 21, 2013, www.latimes.com/world/worldnow/la-fg-wn-ex-pope-benedict-god-told-him-resign-20130821-story.html.

101 *Ask me not where I live*: Thomas Merton, *My Argument with the Gestapo* (New York: New Directions, 1975), loc. 2150, Kindle.

10 FINDING SPIRITUAL FREEDOM

105 *a kind of realized, existential freedom*: John English, *Spiritual Freedom* (Chicago: Loyola Press, 1995), 18.

107 *Many people think*: English, *Spiritual Freedom*, 20.

11 REMEMBER THE SIGNS

111 *Jill and the lion*: This story is adapted from C. S. Lewis, *The Silver Chair* (New York: Macmillan, 1953), 14-18.

114 *Remember, remember, remember*: Lewis, *Silver Chair*, 18-21.

119 *The way up from the depths*: Jane Vennard, *Be Still: Designing and Leading Contemplative Retreats* (Herndon, VA: Alban Institute, 2000), 29. This section relies heavily on pages 29-30 in Vennard's book.

12 IN RETURNING AND REST YOU SHALL BE SAVED

125 *To live a spiritual life*: Henri Nouwen, *Reaching Out: The Three Movements of the Spiritual Life* (New York: Doubleday, 1975), 34.

126 *The main purpose of retreat*: John Oliver Nelson, *Retreats: An Introductory Manual*, ed. Mary Lou Van Buren (Cincinnati: General Board of Global Ministries, 1981), 21.

"The best thing any of us can bring to leadership is our own transforming selves. That is the journey I am committed to and it is the journey to which you are invited as well."

—Ruth Haley Barton

Visit *ruthhaleybarton.com* to

- Discover additional resources written by Ruth
- Listen to Ruth's podcast
- Subscribe to Ruth's blog

Ruth has been a student, practitioner, and leader in the area of Christian spirituality and spiritual formation for over twenty years. Encountering the richness of the broader Christian tradition has led Ruth to reclaim practices and experiences that spiritual seekers down through the ages have used to open themselves to God's transforming work.

Join Ruth on Retreat

A sought-after teacher, preacher, and retreat leader, you will always find Ruth teaching and leading the Transforming Center's two-year Transforming Community experience—a practice-based spiritual formation journey for leaders and influencers offered in nine quarterly retreats. For more information visit transformingcenter.org.

ruthhaleybarton.com

TRANSF●RMINGRESOURCES
A Ministry of the Transforming Center®

More from Ruth Haley Barton

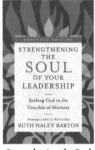

**Strengthening the Soul
of Your Leadership**

**Pursuing God's
Will Together**

Longing for More

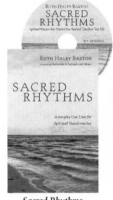

Sacred Rhythms

Sacred Rhythms DVD
curriculum

**Invitation to Solitude
and Silence**

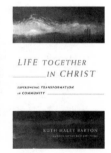

Life Together in Christ

To learn more about transforming resources, communities, and events, visit
transformingcenter.org

TRANSF●RMING CENTER
Strengthening the Soul of Your Leadership

TRANSF**O**RMINGRESOURCES®
A Ministry of the Transforming Center®

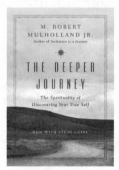

The Deeper Journey

Invitations from God

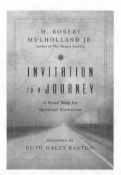

Invitation to a Journey

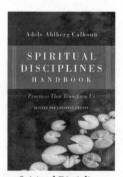

Spiritual Disciplines
Handbook

To learn more about transforming resources, communities, and events, visit
transformingcenter.org

TRANSF**O**RMING CENTER
Strengthening the Soul of Your Leadership